Proven

Proposal

Strategies

to Win More

Business

Herman Holtz

Upstart
Publishing Company
Specializing in Small Business Publishing
a division of Dearborn Publishing Group, Inc.

This publication is designed to provide accurate and authoritative information in regard to the subject matter covered. It is sold with the understanding that the publisher is not engaged in rendering legal, accounting, or other professional service. If legal advice or other expert assistance is required, the services of a competent professional person should be sought.

Acquisitions Editor: Danielle Egan-Miller
Managing Editor: Jack Kiburz
Interior Design: Lucy Jenkins
Cover Design: S. Laird Jenkins Corporation
Typesetting: Professional Resources & Communications, Inc.

Published by Upstart Publishing Company,
a division of Dearborn Publishing Group, Inc.

Printed in the United States of America

98 99 00 10 9 8 7 6 5 4 3 2 1

Library of Congress Cataloging-in-Publication Data
Holtz, Herman.
    Proven proposal strategies to win more business/Herman Holtz.
        p. cm.
    Includes index.
    ISBN 1-57410-088-2 (hardcover)
    1. Proposal writing in public contracting. I. Title.
    HD3860.H643 1998
    658.15'224—dc21   97-48649
                                                                    CIP

Upstart books are available at special quantity discounts to use as premiums and sales promotions, or for use in corporate training programs. For more information, please call the Special Sales Manager at 800-621-9621, ext. 4384, or write to Dearborn Financial Publishing, Inc., 155 N. Wacker Drive, Chicago, IL 60606-1719.

Dedication

To my greatest fan and greatest comfort, Sherrie, an understanding wife, loving companion, and partner in everything that is important in our lives

Other Books by the Author

The Complete Guide to Consulting Contracts, Second Edition
The Consultant's Guide to Getting Business on the Internet
Priced to Sell: The Complete Guide to More Profitable Pricing
The Business Plan Guide for Independent Consultants
The Independent Consultant's Brochure and Letter Handbook
The Complete Guide to Being an Independent Contractor
Computer Consulting on Your Home-Based PC
The Complete Work-at-Home Companion, Second Edition
How to Succeed as an Independent Consultant, Third Edition

ontents

3 Typical Proposal/Contracting Problems   38

4 RFP Strategies   52

8   Presentation Strategies: II   125

Introduction

Organization of This Book

This book is divided into chapters that

1. address specific kinds of problems for which you need to find solutions, and
2. other important matters relating to the development of winning strategies.

There will be little discussion of writing per se, except for some ideas on creating high-impact presentations—presentations that get attention or provide sudden, sometimes dramatic, insights. As this is a how-to book, specific strategies are offered in some cases, and broad approaches or principles for strategy formulation are suggested in other cases.

An index is provided to assist you in using this book as a reference text so that you may look up specific subjects as the need arises.

How Do I Make My Proposals Work for Me?

A good proposal is a power-packed sales presentation. The major objective for creating your proposal—the reason you are willing to spend so much money, time, and effort in writing it—is to persuade a client to award you a contract. As a sales presentation, a proposal justifies its cost only because it is a marketing investment. Unfortunately, most proposal writers are technicians, engineers, executives, and/or professional specialists of one kind or another, but they are rarely experienced marketers. So, while they may write excellent project plans and descriptions, the only sell-power in their proposals is that added by reviewers who are knowledgeable and able marketing experts. No matter how technically excellent your proposed program, your effort comes to nothing if the proposal does not sell the program.

This book will help you make your proposals more effective as sales presentations. You create a top-quality program that will satisfy your client's needs; I will help you make your proposals far more effective by developing knock-their-socks-off sales strategies. Make no mistake about this: Contracts are won by the proposers who employ the most effective sales strategies. All business is won that way. It is why the VHS videocassette recorder-player put the Beta machine out of business, and why Microsoft is as much number one in software for desktop computers as IBM was once number one in mainframe computers, to name just two examples.

More than 35 years pursuing and winning many government and commercial contracts as a corporate executive, a consultant, and an independent contractor convince me that the principal ingredient of success is marketing strategy. I do not refer to an organization's overall marketing strategy here, but to the individual strategy developed for each individual marketing contest—for each proposal required to get a contract. A client with a unique problem that needs a custom-designed program to satisfy that need issues a Request for Proposal (RFP) that explains its needs and invites you to state how you will meet those needs. To you, each contract competition is an individual sales battle that may bear some resemblance to another procurement of an earlier time, but the client usually regards its need as unique and wants a unique solution proposed. (More about RFPs later.) Address each sales effort individually, and invent a unique strategic sales approach to each opportunity.

It may well be a sales problem that an advertising executive presented when he recalled a visit from a prospective new client. The prospect placed two shiny new silver dollars on the advertising executive's desk.

"I am a brewer," he said. "That is my beer," pointing to one silver dollar," and that is my competitors' beer," pointing to the other silver dollar. "I need you to convince the public that this first silver dollar is better than the other silver dollar."

This book teaches you how to persuade the client that your silver dollar is the best silver dollar.

When I was working on my first proposals, I probably mumbled to myself, as do many beginning proposal writers, "I wonder what they really want." I remember being astonished at how difficult it was to understand many of the RFPs that I read. It didn't occur to me that many clients found it difficult to explain—or even understand—their needs and wants. I knew that not everyone writes well, but I was sure that the writers of RFPs were deliberately being coy, and that the challenge was to decipher the language of the RFP and somehow divine what the writer was trying to say—or perhaps trying *not* to say. And so I groaned when yet another RFP proved to be a challenge to my powers of divination, and I believed I needed such powers!

Much later, after the practical education that came of hard work and many disappointments, I learned to welcome and even prefer the hard-to-understand Statement of Work (SOW), the core document of a client's RFP. I think some of my associates were as much perplexed by my preference for almost incoherent SOWs as they were by their own difficulties in deciphering such statements. They obviously did not understand what the challenge of the difficult, let's say impossible, meant to those hard-headed individuals who love intellectual challenges. If you are sparked by challenge, you will find much to relish here. See Chapter 3 for more about the opportunities present in unclear RFPs.

There are reasons, several of them, for the work statements and other elements in RFPs to be so often difficult to follow, let alone comprehend fully on first reading. But there was and is only one reason for my preference for such statements over crystal-clear ones: I have been able to develop the winning proposals that responded to such statements much more often than I won those in which I responded to crystal-clear RFPs (*rare* RFPs, of course), that I think my own and some others' proposal success has or can have some direct relationship to the difficulty in understanding the RFP.

That is a believe-it-or-not kind of statement, of course, but to a large degree, that is what this book is all about. You are going to learn, soon after plunging into these pages, why I have developed that belief and that preference, why I find that the RFP of that kind offers the best opportunities for success, the greatest opportunities to develop the strategies of success. But before we get into that discussion, let's examine what a proposal is so that we are talking about the same thing.

There are several metaphors that could be used to identify or define a proposal. A proposal is a sales presentation, for one. It is written with the hope that it will win a contract. But a proposal is also a contract exhibit. Once, it was a common practice to include in a project contract an "exhibit," usually appended, describing in detail what the contractor agreed to do. With a growing trend toward requiring prospective contractors to submit detailed proposals describing what they agreed to do, such an exhibit rapidly became redundant. It became obvious that a great reduction in paperwork could be achieved by simply incorporating the contractor's proposal in the contract, at least that part of the proposal that describes what the contractor agrees specifically to do. This has become a common practice today, and it is one reason, a most important reason, that clients need a detailed proposal. It is also why, if changes are agreed to in negotiations, the contractor is asked to submit a written amendment to the proposal or a rewritten proposal to document those changes. Thus, a proposal is—becomes—part of the contract, if accepted.

The significance of this is that in writing a proposal you are writing a significant part of the contract—*proposing* a contract, that is. You are committing yourself to perform precisely what you promise in your proposal. That is an excellent reason to think carefully about what you propose and be sure that it is what you are prepared to do and guarantee for the price you quote.

The entire document you prepare as a proposal is usually a document of several parts, identified as sections or chapters. Each has its function to introduce yourself, to explain and sell your approach, to present your credentials, and to describe in detail what you promise to do and produce as an outcome. The section or chapter that describes in detail the specific program you propose as the services that will satisfy the client's needs as described in the RFP, becomes the contractually binding exhibit to the contract.

A typical proposal format includes an introductory section, a section discussing the client's need and exploring the alternatives to solution, the specific program proposed, and the proposer's credentials. In some cases, there may be an entire section on project and contract management, and sometimes there is an appendix or even several appendixes offering useful ancillary documentation. Thus, one or more sections will actually become part of the contract by reference. This saves everyone a great deal of time and labor, reduces cost, and spares the trees that would otherwise have been cut down to create the paper needed to produce the redundancy.

Strategic Marketing Principles and Government Contracts

A large share of the anecdotes used herein to illustrate strategic triumphs come from successful proposals written in pursuit of government contracts, but most of the strategic principles—the strategic *marketing* principles—are applicable to all marketing—government and commercial contracts—and may easily be adapted to the conditions of all commercial business situations.

Negotiated procurement, in the jargon of federal government purchasing, is an old term. It refers to a process of requesting proposals to provide some custom service and then choosing what a government evaluation committee deems to be the best of these. That is then followed by negotiating with the author of the chosen proposal or, in some cases, with the authors of several acceptable proposals, then requesting from each their best and final offer. (This is, of course, an effort to get the best price for the government, and it may be a decisive factor.) Today, the process is called, officially, *competitive proposals*, but the process is the same. The proposal contest is held to determine who has the most acceptable program, and then to negotiate a contract with that proposer, or with the authors of several of the best proposals. In truth, however, in some cases, especially for the small contracts, negotiation is nothing more than an informal telephone conversation to confirm the offer. Still, it goes down as a negotiation, and some contracting officers will conduct more or less formal negotiations for even small contracts. Negotiating strategies are discussed in Chapter 7.

Many businesses, small and large, avoid the pursuit of government contracts for one reason or another, often because their owners and managers believe some of the common myths about the difficulties of doing business with the government. However, more than a quarter million businesses survive primarily or even exclusively on government contracts. In addition to these, thousands of other businesses, especially small ones, owe some significant portion of their annual sales to government contracts. U.S. government agencies comprise the largest and most diverse market in the world. Perhaps they believe the mythology that it is difficult to win government contracts without "connections" or "pull" and that government takes forever to pay its bills. (These are untruths—myths, for the most part—based on a mere tiny kernel of fact, as most myths are.)

The advantages of doing business with the government are many. One is the assurance of payment. (Our government is not in serious danger of becoming bankrupt, despite our fiscal problems and the cries of some extremists.) Another is contracts that can range from the smallest to the greatest, and you can pursue contracts of any size. Also, the process is subject to law, a voluminous body of procurement regulations and other laws that have an impact on procurement by the government. These severely restrict and limit the impact of political influence on awards and protects your right to compete for and win government business. You really do not have to "know somebody" to succeed in this market. (My own success as a small business owner and independent government contractor is proof enough of that.) That is the good news.

The Pain of Proposal Writing

The bad news, for some at least, is that you usually must write a winning proposal to win contracts for anything but standard commodities in products and services. But that is bad news only if you hate to write proposals and consider it too much of an ordeal to suffer in the quest for business. However, for those of us who think it a great opportunity to be able to compete in the enormous market that government procurement represents—more than $200 billion annually by the federal agencies alone, and about twice as much more by the departments and agencies of the other 80,000 state and local governments—this is good news indeed. Despite the exceptions and cynical rationalizations of those who find it necessary to explain their inability to win in the competitions, winners are chosen and contracts awarded on the basis of the proposals because the system makes it difficult for officials to do otherwise. With experience and the accumulation of your own proposal library, proposal writing becomes less and less difficult and less and less expensive.

Sales Strategy

It has been my experience and is my firm opinion that the basis for successful proposals is sales strategy, far more than any other factor, and it is strategy of several kinds: program or technical strategy, competitive strategy, management strategy, cost strategy, presentation strategy, and, finally, capture strategy, which may be any of the previous strategies listed or some combination thereof.

The quest for strategies may be driven by any of several influences stimulating a rush of adrenaline: The normal stimulus of competitive effort, the extra stimulus of a hot contest, and the stimuli of usual or unusual proposal problems, all provide the motivation for marketers to make an intensive search for a strategic angle.

In any case, whatever the need and inspiration for it, strategy is a prime factor accounting for proposal success. In this book, I shall address three objectives relevant to proposal strategy and success:

1. I will reveal many strategies that are or ought to be more or less reliable old standards, with many applications.
2. I will reveal many special strategies that were developed to meet special situations and needs, and which I hope will inspire the imagination of readers to devise strategies to meet their own special needs in future proposal efforts.
3. I will define a number of special problems that one encounters more or less commonly in responding to requests for proposals, and suggest a few ideas for responding to these special problems and solving them without sacrificing the effectiveness of your proposals.

In the course of doing this, this book will offer another useful tool as a spin-off: I will define the typical and special problems one may expect to encounter in responding to RFPs and suggest general solutions for these problems, although I encourage you to seek solutions of your own.

It is not a how-to-write-a-proposal book, although I have written several of that type. It is, instead, a graduate course in proposal writing, in that its focus is on proposal strategies—the more subtle subjects of success in marketing.

I have one final word that I believe is significant and should be stressed: Although this book is written and recommendations made in the structure of pursuing government contracts and on the basis of much successful experience in government contracting, much of it is transferable to marketing in the commercial world. In fact, federal agencies are turning more and more to good commercial practices to expedite government procurement. In either case, humans will evaluate your submissions. This fact offers both challenges and opportunities.

1

Strategies and the Unique Selling Proposition (USP)

Strategies

You use strategies every day in everything you do. To define *strategies* as simply as possible, they are plans or methods for accomplishing a goal. These are usually simple and obvious methods, such as turning to the Yellow Pages or the Internet to find a plumber, placing a classified advertisement in the daily newspaper to sell something, or tacking up announcements around the neighborhood for a garage sale. In fact, these are such obvious and common methods that it would ordinarily not occur to you to dignify them with such an impressive word as *strategies*. That word implies those special, clever, and perhaps ingenious things you do to solve difficult or special problems when the standard approaches are not effective. You might, for example, add an inducement to the those garage-sale announcements, such as the promise of free refreshments or surprise gifts, as a strategy to attract visitors. Or perhaps while developing a proposal, you plan to offer your prospective client some startling innovation.

When you begin to turn to unusual ways and employ special methods, and especially when you see yourself using novel measures to get greater-than-normal results, overcome a problem, or gain a special advantage, is when you begin to think of your methods as strategies.

How do you devise a selling strategy? You may first try clever modifications of some standard procedure to solve a problem. If that doesn't work out, you may develop a completely new—perhaps even revolutionary—idea. An effective strategy may come to you in some blinding flash of inspiration. More often one "develops" a strategy by making it better at each revision. For example, I now use special forms that I designed for my own bookkeeping needs, but I based them on accepted accounting systems and principles by adapting forms from my earliest bookkeeping system. I originally purchased that system at an office supplies store, as many beginning business owners do. No great innovation here, just simple evolution. I became familiar with typical small-business accounting methods and forms; then I changed the forms to suit my needs. Finally I had developed a complete system that was all my own, despite its pedestrian origins. If my needs change, my "strategy" will be to revise and evolve again.

Whether you face a new challenge and know that you need a unique solution, or whether you realize an old method is no longer effective—you get unique solutions by inventing them.

Inspiration and Invention

Everyone can have useful, new ideas. The "blinding flash of inspiration" that presents you with a brilliant new idea is not as sudden or unexpected as it is so often represented. In fact, serious studies based on many interviews with inventors and others who develop new ideas and new devices, show that the emergence of a new idea usually involves three phases of development:

1. Concentration
2. Incubation
3. Inspiration

Concentration. These inventors first tried consciously to get ideas—to find a solution to a problem or develop a new device. This is the first phase, the period of *concentration,* and it continues as long as you have new ideas to turn over and examine or new questions to see if you are seeking the right answer.

Incubation. At some point, this effort must end. You must lay it aside. You suspend work on the problem and go on to other matters. This is *incubation*. You have now turned the problem over to your subconscious mind.

The subconscious mind is a powerful thinking engine, one that never forgets anything and so is able to analyze and synthesize effectively. But communication between the conscious and subconscious minds is neither easy nor direct. Like looking up all relevant topics in reference books or using an Internet search engine, your subconscious gathers information, discards the irrelevant, and synthesizes the relevant into a usable, focused form.

Inspiration. Ultimately—it may be soon or it may take some time—your subconscious mind responds with an idea, an answer. This is inspiration. It happens most often when you are relaxed, not focused on anything special.

An example that everyone experiences occasionally is the struggle to remember something that you ought to remember easily, such as someone's name. After many attempts to recall it, you give up for the moment—even saying, "Oh, well, it will come to me." And sure enough, at some later time, when you are not trying to force the information out, the name suddenly pops into your head.

When you understand the mechanism, you can deliberately make your subconscious work for you. Follow the steps. Try consciously, as long as possible, to find a solution to your problem, then incubate it and wait for inspiration. Hypnosis often is helpful to relax you and allow your subconscious to "report" to your conscious mind.

Innovation

Innovation—doing something new and different—does not necessarily have to wait on inspiration. Selling has a lot in common with advertising. A generally accepted principle of advertising is to first attract a prospect's attention and then convince the prospect he needs what you are selling. But what are good strategies to attract the prospect's attention? In print advertising you may use distinctively stylized or oversize type fonts, cartoons, brilliant colors, and clever puns or witticism. Nonprint advertising gets attention by using sound and motion. But these are obvious and well-known stratagems. But what new and novel methods of getting attention and arousing interest—strategies—can you devise? The Unique Selling Proposition—USP—which we shall discuss shortly, is one such idea for attracting attention and arousing interest. But there are others, and I can come up with a few ideas consciously, without waiting for inspiration to overtake me.

In a challenging situation, such as one that is extraordinarily competitive or requires you try something that has never been done before, your strategy also must be new and different to cope successfully with the need. It takes a different kind of thinking, a courageous and, quite often, bold thinking.

When Charles "Boss" Kettering was hired by Ransom Olds to develop the so-called self-starter motor for the Oldsmobile, Kettering was setting out to do what contemporary engineers "knew" was impossible. Engineering calculations demonstrated that any motor powerful enough to crank an automobile engine would have to be as large as the engine itself or it would overheat and burn out.

Kettering was a competent engineer and he was well aware that there was no way to reverse or nullify the physical fact of a starter motor generating heat. But *overheating* is a relative—not an absolute—term. How much heat is too much? How much heating up is *over*heating? Kettering set about to find the answer to that question, as it applied to developing a self-starter motor. The answer to that question was the key to his invention.

Kettering reasoned that the starter normally is used for only a few seconds. It does heat up a bit in those few seconds, but the starter is usually not used again soon, and so has ample time to cool down before the next use. The starter motor should therefore be able to tolerate a moderate rise in heating, especially if it is deliberately designed to dissipate the heat as rapidly as possible between uses. The engineering fact that a starter motor would create heat, a fact that others thought presented an insurmountable problem, was offset by Kettering's strategy to use another engineering fact—heat can be dissipated.

Innovation often consists of questioning the truth of conventional wisdom: Do we really know what we think we know? Did we ask *all* the right questions?

The Trouble with Conventional Wisdom

Conventional wisdom is that body of established beliefs and "truisms" that exists for and in just about every field of activity in which people engage. When we undertake to do any job, we look first to "how it's always done" or what "they" all do. Unfortunately, too often we look no further than that, at least not until we run into trouble. When I managed an organization doing contract work for one of the NASA space flight centers, I found myself plagued with invoices returned by NASA because the invoices had numerous errors in them. I discovered that almost all the errors were made in the process of posting figures from employees' time cards to a work sheet and then from the work sheet to the invoices.

My immediate question was, "How do we foolproof the work sheet?" On introspection, the question became, "Why do we need a work sheet? Why do we need to double the opportunities for, and probability of, error by transferring the figures twice?"

Of course, my accountant assured me that using a work sheet was "standard practice." This was the conventional wisdom used to justify the system without examining it for its suitability. However, with long established irreverence for the supposed unassailability of time-honored systems and with a basic faith that everything can be improved, I could find neither need nor justification for this traditional practice in this case. So I redesigned our invoice forms so figures were transferred directly from the time cards to the invoices. That solved the problem, and, as an unexpected bonus, reduced the accounting labor required to prepare invoices.

Conventional practice serves its purpose for conventional situations and uses, but there is nothing sacred about it. It is yesterday's wisdom. You know if it does not work to change it. But remember that if it does not work *optimally,* you should change it.

Often, the most important and most effective strategic change you can make to solve a problem is simplification of the system or operation in which the problem appears. Many of the systems we use are overburdened with unnecessary functions and unnecessary steps that often are the cause of unnecessary problems. Always consider simplification through elimination of or combining steps or functions. Besides solving problems, you may get additional benefits such as reduction of costs. Try to develop a general independence of thought, a questioning attitude about how everything is currently being done, and a conviction that everything can be improved. (History provides clear proof of that.) Try, in fact, to employ a few basics of value analysis—a discipline that began life as "value engineering," but as its application spread to fields other than engineering, it became known by the more general terms "value analysis" and "value management" (the latter term favored by some government agencies)—a modern tool for creative thinking and strategic development.

Value Analysis

"Value" is a rather slippery concept because it has many variants, depending on a wide number of qualifying modifiers attached to it. Some kinds of value are intrinsic, market, esteem, historical, and added. Value analysis is a questioning, critical practice of seeking the greatest benefit for the lowest cost. To do this, you ask certain questions of whatever it is that is being subjected to the analysis, which may be a system, a product, a job description, or almost anything that people build or design. The most basic of the questions are the first two, intended to define the item:

1. What is it?
2. What does it do?

The first question must identify the subject of the study with a definitive word, and the second question must respond with a pair of words—a noun and a verb. To keep the description objective, adjectives and adverbs are banned. Let us suppose, for illustration, that the answer to the first question is "pencil." That is an unacceptable answer here. A pencil does not write; people write, using a pencil. Moreover, pencils are also used to draw illustrations, to create guidelines for cutting, and to check off items, to name three other nonwriting functions of the pencil. A more suitable answer is "it makes marks."

The "what does it do?" question addresses the primary function of the item. Value analysis goes on to ask additional questions, such as "what else does it do?" That uncovers secondary functions, if any. Most pencils are equipped with erasers, so the item does do something else: it "removes marks."

"What else would do that?" and "what would it cost?" are additional questions. Not to belabor the point, for the study of value analysis is a lengthy study in itself and so can be treated only briefly here, the questions are pointed and intended to provoke objective analytical examination. Value analysis exposes materials, functions, duties, and other inefficiencies. Value analysis uncovers ways to simplify products, processes, and systems, and so, in a great many cases, increases value. Most important for our purposes here, it guides one in considering all aspects critically and objectively. In so doing, value analysis also forces recognition of different kinds of value. While steel could be used to make jewelry, precious metals have esteem value to consider, a matter not lost on those making value studies. Note the philosophy underlying the practice: Question and demand answers in unemotional, objective terms (especially, the question "what else would do that?"). To enforce objectivity, questions must be answered in two words, a verb and a noun. (Where necessary, one of the "words" may be compounded by additional words.) It is a guide to disciplined reasoning, and the rule of using a noun and verb is intended to compel objectivity.

Boss Kettering had a word of his own to say about the thinking process in general. Although he was especially noted for inventing that automotive self-starter, he had many other accomplishments to his credit, for he was an inventive genius. He was, in fact, a truly independent, creative thinker, and a champion of education. But much as he prized education, he endorsed education with the proviso that education and independent thinking are not the same thing. Education is valuable, he stated, but it must not replace or be permitted to hinder independent thinking. And effective strategies are, of course, the products of independent and innovative thinking, the search for another, better way, often at the cost of casting out the old and familiar. A stubborn and unreasonable clinging to the old and familiar is a symptom of insecurity. Embracing the new and untried idea is risky, both because of the distinct possibility of failure and because it almost always draws fierce objections and ridicule from less imaginative observers. It thus takes courage to be an independent thinker and innovator. You must somehow find that courage, as Edison, Fulton, Copernicus, Pasteur, and other independent thinkers throughout history had to do. Nor has the situation changed in more modern times. Even young Montgomery Ward had to endure and survive a great deal of sneering, jeering criticism, and angry opposition to his innovative business idea of the unconditional guarantee (discussed later under "The Unique Selling Proposition (USP)").

Writing and Its Impact on Proposal Effectiveness

In proposal writing, good sales and marketing presentations win contracts. Fluent language and clear use of language helps, of course, but it is marketing that wins the contract.

Still, do not neglect the importance of writing. Even the most potent sales arguments and marketing strategies will not be effective if they are not well executed—made clear to the reader and presented effectively. And, of course, the instruments of the presentation are written instruments. Some RFPs have page limitations so writing skills assume a special importance. What makes writing effective or ineffective? What *writing strategies* work well to make writing effective in achieving its goals?

First of all, perfection in the mechanics—grammar, punctuation, and spelling, for example—do not ensure quality writing. They are simply the tools, as a wrench and blow torch are tools of plumbing. But knowing how to use the tools does not make you a writer any more than knowing how to use the tools makes you a plumber. A good plumber with poor tools will do a better job than a poor plumber with good tools.

Poor writing is often the result of a writer who does not understand or comprehend the material well enough and who therefore circles the subject uncertainly, often writing verbosely but saying little. The result is lengthy circumlocutions and evasions. Be aware when you are evading coming to grips with the subject. Return to preparation for writing—researching your material—to correct the problem.

One strategy that helps to reveal the need for more research is to use the noun-verb strategy of value analysis. Eliminate modifiers—adjectives and adverbs—and stick to unadorned nouns and verbs. This will not only make your writing more direct and forceful, but also help you recognize that you are not yet ready to write because you have not yet mastered the subject. Try to write about any subject, using only nouns and verbs, or edit all the adjectives and adverbs out of something you already have written. Notice how this focuses your style. Do a self-appraisal of your writing using this method. Note how this exercise raises your awareness of how often writers tend to overuse modifiers and even to rely on them to conceal a lack of preparation and readiness for writing.

Another exercise to test your readiness to write is to explain a complex or technical subject in lay language, abandoning all technical jargon. This puts your own understanding of the subject to the test. If you truly understand your subject, you ought to be able to explain it in simple everyday language If you cannot do this, take it as a sign that you need to master your subject before writing further.

Another reason for writing badly is writing without a clear objective. Writing is done for some purpose, such as to explain, to argue a point, to persuade, or to reveal something. In a proposal, we are usually trying to do each of these things at different points in the presentation. But you must have a clear idea of what you are trying to do at each step. Here, for example, I am trying to explain what I believe is the cause of bad writing and show how you can improve the quality of your writing. I am writing a how-to—not a philosophy—and so I must be direct and simplify everything possible in my explanations. There is no logic or rationale required here, as that would be an argument.

An important part of the objective is knowing to whom you are writing. In one section of your proposal, you may be addressing a design engineer with technical information, whereas in another section you are addressing a field engineer with maintenance information, and in still another area you are writing for a logistics specialist. You must be clear on these things, if your writing is to do its job well (i.e., to make your points and be convincing).

Bear these points in mind, as we proceed, for they will support your understanding of other points made in these pages.

The Unique Selling Proposition (USP)

A Unique Selling Proposition (USP) is a strategy for selling by offering something special that no one else offers—a unique benefit or feature. A USP lends itself well to being a device for attracting attention and generating interest.

Montgomery Ward's USP was the offer of an unconditional, no-questions-asked, money-back guarantee for his customers. Of course, by definition, a USP can exist only as long as it is, in fact, unique. Self-service was once a USP, as was free home delivery, the supermarket, in-store shopping carts, and many other innovations that are in common use today. As you can see, most USPs are thus perishable; something lasts as a USP only as long as only one individual or organization offers it. Ironically, the more successful a USP, the shorter will be its unique life. Certainly the most effective ones are transient, for competitors will always imitate success. Standard Oil Company's founder, John D. Rockefeller, openly advocated emulation of others' successful ventures as a business policy, and he was not alone in that thinking. You may count on every really good idea someone develops being adopted and imitated by others very soon. (Rockefeller also appreciated the importance of independent thought, however, and once counseled one of his young employees to slow down occasionally and take the time to lean back and think about how the company could be run more profitably.) In addition, surprisingly often the same idea occurs to two people almost simultaneously, as in the case of radio and other important inventions. The state of knowledge in one or more areas reaches a point where the next step is truly "an idea whose time has come."

Technically, "unique" does not mean just rare, but means one-of-a-kind in the entire universe. For the purpose of creating a USP, it is the customer's perception that is important. So it is the customer's perception that an item is unique because no one else offers it or, if they do offer it, they fail to announce it, that makes a USP. That marketing strategy is why so many advertisements claim exclusivity of one kind or another, such as "biggest sale ever," "only Blank Company can offer you this," "a genuine Blank toolbox," and other such efforts to stand out from the crowd by offering something unique.

Of course, many of these kinds of offerings are not true USPs because they are only vague claims, and they do not even suggest—much less specify—a unique benefit to the customer. To win customers, the USP must be prominently and clearly stated. Customers will normally not make the important connection between the USP and their personal interests, so you must make the connection for them

In writing proposals to one government agency, I was told that it was not necessary for me to furnish so much detail about my organization's credentials because we were already so well known and respected. I continued the practice anyway because I believe we must assume that the reader of a proposal knows only what the proposal says specifically. It is hazardous to assume otherwise. The individual reading your proposal may be a new employee who has never heard of you. In evaluating government proposals, reviewers are not permitted to infer anything, but can credit your proposal only for what it specifically presents, no matter how well they know you. Failure to understand that has cost more than one proposer a contract award. Always provide all details as specifically as possible and as completely as possible.

For example, in proposing a design for a teleprinter to be used aboard ship by the U.S. Navy, the successful bidder became convinced that all his competitors were going to propose a system built around their own commercial items so that their proposed teleprinters would each be made up of several independent components connected to constitute a system, much as one sets up a stereo system comprised of multiple units. The successful proposer planned to build a special unit housing everything. The advantages of using such a design for equipment to be used aboard ship, where so much has to be fastened down in some way, were obvious enough. However, in the successful proposal, this was pointed out specifically as a major advantage to make sure the customer did not miss the point. To dramatize their design and its benefits as a USP, the successful company repeatedly characterized their unit as a "monolithic" one. "Monolithic" became the USP for that product in its proposals. The client was soon tuned in to the message, and the design of all competing models suffered by comparison with the monolithic design, which was now virtually an accepted standard of the right way to build a shipboard teleprinter!

It should be evident now that a USP can be almost any kind of feature—a kind of guarantee, a characteristic of the product, the cost, the type of contract, the method of payment, a function, a bonus feature, the length of time for which the offer is firm, or almost anything else, as long as it is unique and delivers an *important* benefit. A client in the training business, for example, found that all his competitors offered to supply experienced instructors. The client, however, offered to supply experienced instructors who *also* were experts in the subjects being trained. The USP then was that they would serve as both instructors and consultants by answering customer-specific questions and offering advice on matters not covered in the training manuals and related materials. He could thus use such slogans as, "Our instructors are also consultants to our clients" or variations on that theme.

Used correctly, the USP serves more than one function. It is both a competitive strategy and the basis for commanding attention and arousing interest.

USP Benefits

The benefits of a USP are sometimes clear enough in the description or identification of the USP and need merely be pointed out to the prospect. Some USPs, however, do not themselves telegraph their benefits. In offering such a USP, therefore, you must determine exactly what the most important benefit is to the customer and point it out. In one case, for example, our team was proposing to be the contractors for an elaborate and extensive logistics system for the U.S. Army Corps of Engineers for a major construction program in the Middle East. The flowchart we developed to reveal all the phases of the program and functions we proposed to carry out was six feet long! Additionally, the program required that all procurement, storage, packing, shipment, and receiving be computer documented, plus that all proper paper-and-ink reports and official forms be made up and placed in the record as well.

To avoid creating two more six-foot charts to reflect the accompanying computer events and the paper trail, the team hit on the scheme of creating three parallel charts on one sheet. The original flowchart of logistics events proceeding left to right across the middle of the sheet, the corresponding computer track above it, and the paper trail below it. Events on each track were correlated in function and phase. The concept is illustrated in Figure 1.1 in simplified form. The events are thus correlated neatly to make clear both function and phase relationships among the events in the three streams of related activities.

The benefit to the customer and the customer's reaction was as unexpected as it was pleasing: The customer said that after studying the chart, he now fully understood his own program for the first time! (The same thing could be said for our own team members.)

This is an example of serendipity. Our purpose was to avoid having three unwieldy charts. The benefits in both the aid it gave the writers of the proposal and the presentation's affect on the customer were fortunate by-products. In fact, the greater lesson was that of having helped the customer better understand his own problem and need. Having learned that, the members of this proposal team became most conscious of the need to develop such special presentations for complex requirements and advising proposal readers that great pains were being taken to make a complex program more readily understood by the customer, as well as by themselves.

There was one more step we took to magnify the beneficial affect of that six-foot chart. Although it was a part of the proposal as a foldout chart, we mounted the original copy of the chart on stiff art board, hinging it in the middle so that it could be easily transported, and delivered it to the client along with the proposal. The client could set up the chart as a display for ready reference during proposal reading and any discussions the client's team of evaluators held about the proposal.

This large visual aid delivered with the proposal was a kind of USP that we found to be useful strategically on a number of occasions.

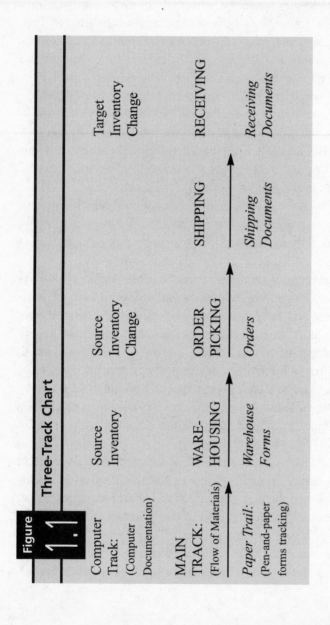

Figure 1.1 Three-Track Chart

	Source Inventory	Source Inventory Change		Target Inventory Change
Computer Track: (Computer Documentation)				
MAIN TRACK: (Flow of Materials)	WARE-HOUSING	ORDER PICKING	SHIPPING	RECEIVING
Paper Trail: (Pen-and-paper forms tracking)	Warehouse Forms	Orders	Shipping Documents	Receiving Documents

The Short Life of a USP

The presentation strategy of three parallel tracks on a single fold-out flowchart was an effective USP, but like Montgomery Ward's unconditional guarantee, it had a short life, although for a different reason. In Ward's case, the life of his USP was short because overwhelming embracing of the unconditional guarantee by Ward's customers compelled his competitors to adopt and offer a similar guarantee. While the policy continued, it was no longer unique. For the flowchart, the USP had a limited life because it was designed for a specific situation. The idea of furnishing a large visual aid to assist in digesting the proposal and for other relevant use is still valid and useful in many other applications.

The existence of a single, specialized need is inherent in the nature of proposal writing. The typical proposal request calls for a custom-designed strategy to meet a special need. A USP developed for that proposal will fit no other need or proposal directly, although it may be adaptable to similar problems. Here are at least two good reasons for not trying to come up with a standardized USP that will fit many proposals:

1. If you try to devise a standard USP, you compromise your dedication to finding a unique solution for a unique problem or need.
2. A USP that you have made standard enough to use over and over is one that your competitors can imitate and adapt to their own uses. Your USP is nullified as something unique or noteworthy, let alone of decisive importance.

While each proposal requires its own USP developed from scratch to fit that proposal, you can utilize the idea of an earlier USP as a seed from which a new USP may be germinated. Although we may never again have occasion to create a three-track functional flowchart for a complex program of many functions, there is no reason that we should not make good use of the idea of a wall chart of our proposed program as a visual aid in reading and understanding a proposal. Study every USP you use (or see) to find possible variations to give it new and vigorous life for another proposal.

You may have standardized distinctive logos, slogans, or other distinguishing features in your proposal. You may, in fact, have several USPs creating strategies for various considerations—technical features, costs, ancillary services, or other—but there is some risk in having too many goodies in any sales argument: Minor goodies must be kept in the background and not confused with the major USP. It is far better not to mention them at all than to risk their stealing the spotlight from your principal USP—the one that focuses on a matter important enough to your customer to be decisive in the final award decision. Do not distract or confuse the proposal reader as to precisely what it is that is the chief promise and proof upon which your claim to the contract is based. Remember always that a proposal is a sales presentation, and you must keep your client's attention focused on what you are offering.

In checking back on proposals that did not win contracts, despite being strong contenders, I found that in some cases their failure was not in quality but due primarily to being less distinctive and memorable than some competitive proposal. Remember that the evaluation process is never quite as objective as the system was designed to make it. Despite evaluation criteria and mandated evaluative processes, human judgment, with all its weaknesses of subjectivity and subconscious bias, is a major factor, finally, and must be considered in devising your strategies. Commanding attention and making your proposal a distinctive and memorable one is of great importance and may very well be a decisive factor.

Be Sure That Your USP *Is* a USP

In finding or creating a new USP for every proposal, bear in mind the two important characteristics that are absolutely necessary to make the USP effective:

1. It must be something that will get attention, is not being offered elsewhere, and will make your offering distinctive and memorable. (Without these characteristics, it does not merit being

called a USP at all.) The effective USP is not modest, but bold and assertive.

2. It must offer the client a benefit important enough to influence his or her decision to award you the contract. Doing anything less wastes your time in writing the proposal and the reader's time in considering it.

In the Beginning: The Preproposal Stage

2

This chapter mainly addresses preproposal activities and strategies for getting the greatest benefits from activities that take place before actual proposal writing begins, although in many cases there may not be a sharp dividing line between preparing to write a proposal and beginning the actual writing. For many reasons, the process usually is not sequential. One of those reasons is that proposal development is usually an *ad hoc* function with an *ad hoc* team assembled, too often on the basis of who can be spared, rather than who is best qualified to write the proposal. The writing is not sequential because each person writes what she knows. This lack of planning leads to a problem in flow and cohesiveness.

Incidentally, use of the term *proposal development,* rather than *proposal writing,* is deliberate, and is connected with the idea of strategies as decisive factors in pursuing contracts. The careless use of the term *proposal writing* leads many to the mistaken notion that proposal development is principally a writing discipline, and that therefore writing is the chief skill needed for writing an effective proposal.

Chapter 1 discussed why writing skill alone will not create an effective proposal and what you need to create a skillful presentation. Keep these points in mind while still maximizing the fluency and effectiveness of your writing.

Where Strategic Thinking Must Begin

This chapter contains many ideas and examples of strategic initiatives that won contracts—government and commercial—as well as explanations of how each strategy was inspired and developed. Many of the strategies were unique, and were developed to handle unique needs. Other strategic concepts are ideas that fit, or can be made to fit, many situations. You can use them again and again, with or without adaptation to the individual case. Here is where it is important to dig down into your own consciousness for some creative inspiration. A small twist of an earlier stratagem may transform it completely into a new strategy that will win an important new contract.

In the process of responding to an RFP, when does one choose or develop a strategy? Is it when you are initially reading and trying to analyze the stated requirement and description of the need or problem the client is presenting? When you are devising a program to propose? When you are drafting your proposal? When you are making final revisions to your proposal? Or at some other time during that lengthy process from opening the envelope containing the RFP to signing the letter of transmittal and sealing the package for delivery?

The answer is *yes* to each of the listed options. Proposal strategies may evolve at any time—before you begin to plan your program or even before you decide to respond with a proposal or a no-bid letter (one explaining that you will not be sending a proposal for this project but want to be retained on the bidders list for future RFPs; a no-bid letter is not required but should be sent). The possible strategies that occur to you at this point may themselves be important factors in your bid/no-bid decision. However, there are other important strategies to consider. They are the strategies that enter into preproposal planning and proposal management, such as perceiving some advantages you have by virtue of special experience closely related to the work called for or some circumstance that holds the promise of providing a cost advantage.

Understanding General Sales Strategy

A proposal is, of course, a sales presentation, and so proposal strategies are inevitably sales strategies. This is why an understanding of sales principles is at least as important as are writing skills in developing successful proposals. Three truths that are the foundation of the art of selling are also basic principles in the selling arts of persuasion and motivation:

1. Customers (and people in general) act much more out of emotional drives than out of logic and reason, although they often use logic and reason to rationalize their buying decisions.
2. Truth, for sales and marketing purposes, is whatever the customer perceives or can be persuaded to perceive as truth.
3. What you sell are promises—promises to *do* something for the customer.

Promises and Perceptions: The Role of Emotion

As semanticists say, the word is not the thing. And what one sells to a client is also not the thing; it is a promise. Your proposal should promise to produce certain results, and explain how you will achieve those results. The client does or does not buy that promise, and a major part of your proposal must be devoted to motivating the customer to buy it. The promise must be something the customer would like to believe (i.e., a benefit that is important to the customer) and you must include information that convinces the customer that you or your service or product can and will make good on the promise.

The principle is true for whatever you sell. People buy what they perceive the product or service will do for them. A customer who buys some tangible object—something one can see, feel, taste, or smell—is still buying what you promise that object is.

That is why sales trainers urge selling the promises of benefits, not features. That is selling the promise of what the product or service *does*, not what it *is*: Customers buy the promises of sparkling clean dishes and glassware without streaks, your friends' envy and admiration of your new jewelry, visions of enhanced beauty and sex appeal cosmetics will confer on you, the satisfaction and pride of driving a stylishly expensive new automobile, or the sense of security of an insurance policy. It is this emotional appeal that supersalesman Elmer Wheeler referred to when he uttered what became one of the most publicized phrases in the art of selling: "Sell the sizzle, not the steak." He also said, "If you want to sell lemonade, you must make your customers thirsty." The concept was that of creating a want, a need. Elmer Wheeler was referring to a sales situation where there is not yet a *felt need*, a need of which the prospect is already conscious. So Wheeler was suggesting the use of emotional appeals to create the needs by helping the prospect develop a desire for the product or benefit.

In the case of most proposals (and all those that are submitted in response to a Request for Proposal), the need already exists in the client's mind. But it is a need for some service or product the client envisions in general. Your job, in developing your proposal, is to sharpen the view the client has of his or her general need by making it a perception of a special need for the benefit from the individual product or service that *you* offer.

From now on, as you read, view, and hear advertisements and commercials, note the emotional appeal stated or implied. Note also how often the promise of economy or low price is a secondary promise, not the primary one. If you can find a powerful enough primary purpose, you do not need to rely on a low-cost strategy as your primary motivator. (Studies reveal that price is not the primary reason for most purchases.) As you proceed, see how often positioning yourself as *the* provider of a benefit creates winning strategies for all kinds of sales situations.

The Need for Evidence: The Role of Reason

"Selling the sizzle" does not mean that customers do not employ some reasoning in their decisions. They do, of course, especially in rationalizing and justifying their buying decisions. However, emotion is powerful enough to overcome reason (or at least temper it considerably). The more powerful the emotion—the more powerful the client's *want* or emotional desire for the benefit promised—the more it dominates the client's motivation and final decision.

No matter the emotional motivation, that great desire to enjoy the benefits promised by the proposer, the customer still finds it necessary to exercise some reason, to rationalize the buying decision. The clever salesperson provides the rationalization by showing you that the overpriced red sports car that has won your love keeps its value and so is really an investment. Do you believe that? You do if you want to believe it enough, if you want to justify the purchase to yourself, and if the evidence offered to support the promise appears to be reasonable enough.

In practice, the emotional appeal has two major elements: promise and proof. Promise is the principal benefit offered, the emotion-based appeal to achieve some desirable end for the customer. Proof is whatever acceptable evidence you offer to prove you can and will deliver on your promise. What you offer is *acceptable* evidence if, and only if, the client accepts it as evidence or proof. Again, the client's *perception* determines whether what you offer is or is not proof.

Strategic Concerns of the Bid/No-Bid Study

Even the most ambitious and most aggressive contractors do not respond to every RFP with a proposal. They study the RFP to decide whether they will respond or decline to do so. In making the preproposal analysis of the RFP to decide whether you will respond with a proposal or a no-bid letter, you should usually consider at least the following points and perhaps others not mentioned here:

- Is the work called for consistent with the kind of work you normally do? Do you already have the necessary know-how, the staff, and the facilities or would you have to reorganize and possibly refit to handle this?
- Do you have room in your present schedule to take this job on and give it your full attention? Could you manage this project, along with what you now have in progress and are committed to?

- What are your advantages, if any, general or special, vis-à-vis winning and completing this project successfully?
- What are your disadvantages, if any, general or special, vis-à-vis winning and completing this project successfully?
- What do you estimate your chances of winning the contract to be?
- What is your current backlog and workload? How badly do you need a new contract in the near future?
- What is the upside of taking on this contract? (Growth potential? Profits? Other?)
- What is the downside of taking it on? (Diluting your effectiveness on existing projects? Heavy new burdens? Other?)

Strategic Concerns of the Preproposal Conference

Frequently, the client will conduct a preproposal conference to which all who were sent an RFP are invited. The purpose is to provide more detailed explanations of the client's need than the RFP provided, to get a better insight into contractors' views of the problems, and to answer any questions in an open forum so that all interested parties can hear the answers. Sometimes this conference was preplanned and the invitation included in the original RFP letter. On other occasions, the client has received many questions after issuing the RFP, and therefore decides that a preproposal conference is necessary to answer questions and clarify the need.

What Not to Do at Preproposal Conferences

Attendance and judicious behavior at a preproposal conference should be governed by strategic considerations of your own:

- Should you ask questions of the client to get a better understanding of the requirement?
- Should you comment or amplify on others' questions, clarify them further, suggest answers, or pose follow-up questions?

- Should you take advantage of the occasion to let the client know who you are—to become more recognizable to the client and possibly impress the client with your knowledge and expertise?

These may seem to be sensible and desirable things to do, but my answer to all these questions is an emphatic *No!* Your strategy at a preproposal conference is to listen and to learn, not to talk or give away information. Observe who else is in attendance. Careful listening may provide you with some useful information beyond what you can find in the RFP. On the other hand, talking—asking questions and getting a few answers—may help some others there, but it probably will not help you. Most preproposal conferences attract many eager hopefuls, attendees having little relevant knowledge or ability vis-à-vis the procurement, but who are there with the hope that they will somehow glean enough to make the trip worthwhile and perhaps even enable them to make a try at the contract. A surprisingly large number of people make earnest tries at winning contracts for work they know very little about. Your questions and the answers they bring may come as helpful education to some of those present and encourage—perhaps even strengthen them—as competitors. Attendees at the conference who are as experienced and capable as you in the work and in proposal competitions generally, are your most serious competition for the contract. Why reveal your thinking to them at this early point?

Strategies that will be discussed later will further illustrate why silence is well advised for most cases, and how to turn uncertainties, weaknesses in the RFP, and unanswered questions about the RFP, into decisive assets.

What to Do at Preproposal Conferences

If the above is what not to do at a preproposal conference, what are the things you should do? Consider these items:

- Judging by the questions you hear being asked, how many of those present are serious competitors? How many are from competitive organizations? How many are eager hopefuls but not true competitors? How many will not propose, but are in attendance because they are marketing specialists and attend all events that are even remotely connected with their normal interests?

- Identify as many organizations represented at the conference as you can. You may know some of the individuals from earlier occasions. Some who make comments or ask questions may identify their organizations in so doing. There may be a sign-in sheet you can look at, or the client may be willing to furnish a list of attendees later. Take advantage of this, along with what you have been able to deduce from listening to others' questions, to help you estimate how many proposals are likely to result—that is, how much competition you may expect and who your major competitors are likely to be.

- Try to ascertain the client's worry items, those things about which the client appears most concerned, such as the cost, the schedule, the quality, the feasibility of satisfying the need, or the credentials of the contractor. Addressing the client's fears can be a winning strategy.

- Chat with others, especially any individuals you happen to know, listening for clues as to their reactions to the solicitation or anything they know about the requirement or the client. Be noncommittal about your own intentions or ideas.

Whatever you glean at the preproposal conference helps you with your own bid/no-bid decision, even though you would probably not yet have decided whether or not to propose.

Strategic Concerns in Reading the RFP

At this point, you have read the RFP, but presumably have not yet studied it seriously. Studying it seriously means poring over it many times, reading what is between the lines, as well as what is in the lines. I have often found it necessary to read and reread an RFP a dozen times to get what I wanted out of it. On some notable occasions, it has been the last reading that provided the clue for the winning strategy. As in the modern jest about computers, when all else fails, read the instructions. The clue you need so badly is not always in the Statement of Work, but that is the first place to look for it. If you still do not have a firm grasp of the client's needs, your clue may be found in other parts of the bid package, so give these your full attention too.

Lists That Help You Make an RFP Analysis

It is not necessary to rely on your mental juggling of ideas alone to make a complete, thorough, and useful analysis. In fact, if you follow the procedures for RFP analysis below, your study also should help you accomplish several other useful tasks:

- It will point to items or considerations that concern, or ought to concern, the client. Identifying clients' concerns will help you focus your proposal.
- It will expose weaknesses in the RFP: anomalies, contradictions, gaps in necessary information, and other faults, as clues to help you address worry items your client has not identified.
- It may suggest one or more strategies, especially the capture or main strategy.
- It may help you determine the structure of the proposal and/or give you strong clues as to what it is you ought to include in your program.

Some items may leap off the page as you read, but it is unlikely that you will detect or infer all the important items from reading alone—even from multiple readings. You will be wise to reread the RFP several times during the course of proposal development, as questions arise in your mind and you return to the RFP to see if there are clues there you missed or did not appreciate in earlier readings. To be sure you do not miss something important, you need some aids. The first one is a set of three checklists that you should construct as you read and reread the RFP (see Figure 2.1).

Figure 2.1	Sample RFP Checklist (cross-referenced to the RFP)

PROJECT REQUIREMENTS	PROPOSAL REQUIREMENTS	EVALUATION CRITERIA
Turnkey operation (para. 3.1)	Résumé of contract administrator (para. 5.4)	Understanding of requirement (para. 7.2)
Training program (para. 4.2)	State financial resources (para. 5.6)	Staff credentials (para. 7.3)
Validation testing (para. 4.6)	State schedule compliance (para. 5.9)	Relevant company experience (para. 7.8)
Special skills (para. 4.9)	List of deliverables (para. 5.3)	Management control (para. 7.9)
Operations manual (para. 5.1)	Training materials (para. 4.4)	Validation program (para. 7.10)

- List 1: Project requirements list all the information items that the RFP makes clear are required as specific information in your proposal.
- List 2: Proposal requirements list all the specific items that are required to be included and described in your proposed program.
- List 3: Evaluation criteria list those items that will be scored specifically in awarding the proposal a technical rating.

(Lists should be drawn up in a manner that facilitates the construction of matrixes as discussed in Chapter 9.)

Evaluation criteria require some explanation: Federal RFPs include an explanation of the criteria that will be weighed in assigning your technical proposal a score, called a figure of merit. Sometimes these evaluation criteria are described quite specifically and in great detail. In other cases their description is somewhat sketchy, so you may have to make some educated guesses from what is said on the subject.

Nonfederal proposals usually will not specify the evaluation criteria, so you will have to judge for yourself which are the most important items to the client. It is wise to make up this list, even if it is one of inferences and not specific information from the RFP. At the least, its existence will prompt you to consider the important subject of proposal evaluation for technical merit. (In fact, it is not amiss to list these items in your proposal with the argument that these are the factors that make your proposal the right one for the requirement. I have even found it useful, on some occasions, to describe for the client what I consider to be the necessary contractor qualifications for success.)

You may wish to make a fourth list, a list of worry items or items you believe to be good candidates for development into worry items. However, since this would probably be a short list, you will probably manage well by marking such items on the lists where they already appear.

There may be items or strengths that occur to you but do not fall in these lists. You may want to consider making notes at this time, while the ideas are fresh in your mind, for use later in writing your proposal. My own experience is that I will forget items of importance if I do not do something to make notes of them when they occur to me. (I usually work at my computer, and I make notes in a special file to which I can and do refer frequently in the course of writing the proposal. When I use an item in the proposal, I change it to italic in this file so when I am finished, I know I covered every item.)

Lists serve more than one purpose. Not only are they valuable aids to analysis and something of a guarantee that you will become aware of every item you need to consider in writing your proposal, but they become a checklist you can use to ensure that your proposal is, indeed,

100 percent responsive. In Chapter 9 we will discuss the use of this list in preparing a response matrix as front matter to provide evidence to the client that your proposal is, indeed, 100 percent responsive.

Despite creating lists as a 100 percent reflection of the RFP, you may yet need more help. Even with those lists and your intensive study, you are still trying to visualize the requirement and the program you are going to create to satisfy the requirement. You can use some help in doing this, and that help can be furnished most effectively by creating a functional flowchart (see below). It is a companion piece to the lists, and the two should track together, at least with respect to the required elements of the program proposed. In fact, the two—lists and functional flowchart—are mutually supportive, both in development and subsequent use.

The Functional Flowchart

The functional flowchart is something like a map: It shows the reader how to get there from here—the route to the desired end result from whatever starting point has been identified.

The creation of a first-draft functional flowchart is relatively easy when the RFP is at least fairly well detailed, complete, and logical in its flow. In many such cases, you could work improvements into the chart even as you are sketching the initial draft. However, from a strategic viewpoint, it is usually a better and more fruitful idea to first translate the RFP directly into a flowchart, ignoring for the moment any flaws you detect. You will refine it later, but with the RFP faithfully represented, you now have some excellent source material for identifying worry items, weaknesses, or logical flaws in what the RFP describes, each of which is a basis for a potential winning strategy.

Unfortunately, often enough an RFP is not sufficiently clear and detailed or well organized enough to lend itself to this first step. In such cases, even with a group of experts assembled to brainstorm together, getting a chart developed can be a laborious and time-consuming task. This is especially the case in the beginning stage, before the chart has even a rudimentary form. Once a pattern begins to emerge, the task becomes much easier.

The Card Trick

One great aid to building a chart in such circumstances, especially to getting the overall shape outlined quickly, is to use "the card trick"—a set of index cards with a step or function written on each card. That is, each card represents one of the boxes that will appear on the chart.

The cards allow you to rearrange the chart as necessary. The cards introduce great fluidity into the development process. You can insert new steps, rearrange the sequence, indicate parallel or subordinate functions, and otherwise make modifications and improvements to the evolving chart.

The sequence of presentation I advocate is horizontally from left to right, and vertically from the top of the page to the bottom. This is the natural path for all of us because that is how we learned to read. A simple flowchart showing the sequence of steps for carrying out a simple project to conduct a survey for a client is:

Plan Survey => Collect Data => Analyze Data => Write Report

Of course, a project this simple does not require a chart to understand, but there is a great deal more to the project than what is shown here. This chart does not show functions, and does not describe how the job is to be done or what are the client's specific requirements. These are merely the four phases of work. You will have to decide how to go about carrying out the work in each phase, complying with the RFP and showing the details in your chart.

A flowchart can take many forms and shapes. It often is enhanced artistically by proposal teams, but the simple block diagram is adequate, and will be used for purposes of illustration here. Figure 2.2 is a sample of such a chart, a bit more detailed than the introductory sample above, but still a simple series of phases, with general functions indicated. This flow of information happens to represent the major phases of typical proposal preparation, as advocated here. Start with the bid/no-bid analysis block in the upper left corner and follow the arrows to complete steps until you reach the lower right-hand corner, where the final report is produced. In practice, such charts are generally reproduced on a sheet long enough to present the entire flow in a single horizontal line, made into a foldout page in the proposal. (Technical manuals and texts, such as those on engineering subjects, frequently have many such drawings in foldout pages.)

The process of constructing a flowchart of the RFP is itself a learning experience, one that enforces a complete understanding of the work

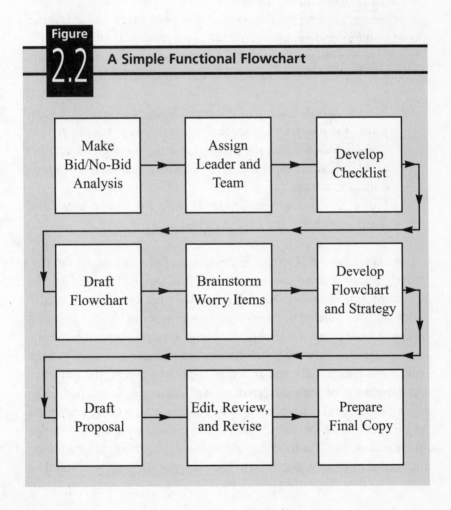

Figure 2.2   A Simple Functional Flowchart

called for by the RFP. Thus, the art of developing the chart is itself a valuable proposal tool, just as the chart itself will be. However, it is not an alternative to developing the checklists; the checklists and the flowchart complement each other, and each helps you make the most of the other. The lists are a great aid to the development of the flowchart, although it is possible to draft the flowchart first from the information presented in the RFP. The two exercises, but especially the development of the flowchart, are a most effective self-imposed education, especially when the project is large and complex. As you will see, each time you do this, the experience gives you an insight into the client's need and the right solution, an insight that you probably could not have gotten otherwise. The development of the chart gives you a graphic, easy-to-understand explanation or interpretation of the RFP. Visualizing the project from just the words of the RFP may be more difficult. Other benefits from creating a flowchart include:

- In a visual presentation of this sort, all major elements are identified, and phase and functional relationships are defined.
- You can often detect the errors, anomalies, gaps, and/or other problems much more easily and clearly than when working only with words.
- Flowcharts make it easier to identify the worry items and develop program and cost strategies.

In many cases, it is almost impossible to fully understand the customer's needs without creating a flowchart. An RFP issued by the Environmental Protection Agency presented such a problem. The RFP called for a contractor to provide an on-site team to run the agency's computers and carry out a large number of specified activities for one of its programs. However, the relationship of these activities to each other, both functionally and in terms of phase—that is, the sequence and correlation of their occurrence—was unclear. I was called on to assist the technical team of a minority contractor in writing a proposal for this project. Fortunately, while I have a good working knowledge of computers, I am far from expert, especially regarding programming and related matters. A good test of the clarity of the proposal would be my ability to understand the requirement and the presentation. I therefore requested that the team first lay the project out as a sequence of functions in a rough flowchart so that I could gain a better understanding of the requirement.

It became obvious very quickly that no one on the proposal team had a clear notion of the proper system configuration as described in the RFP. It seemed evident, in fact, that the client had not thought out the system very clearly either. (In fact, we agreed that if the RFP reflected the client's understanding of the current situation at the EPA, it was clear that this client needed help quite urgently.) Each activity was described well enough, in and of itself, but the system configuration was unclear (if these events and functions actually constituted a system at all). The team spent an entire day discussing and arguing their opinions as to what the RFP said and what it called for. During the same day we developed a rough flowchart to represent our agreement on what the requirement was and what had to be done to satisfy it with a logical, practicable system that we could promise the client would satisfy his need. One senior member of the team stood at the blackboard, chalk in hand, while all discussed each block, and I asked the dumb questions. However, once a rough flowchart was created and agreed on by all the experts, the refinement of the chart and the system it represented became possible, and writing of a successful proposal based on that flowchart proceeded without interruption from that point on.

Because it appeared reasonably certain that the client was himself not at all clear on just what was needed—the clearest thing in the RFP was that the current system was not working—we decided on a strategy of introducing the client to the proposed system with a preliminary illustration, a simplified flowchart that was pictorial, rather than schematic, and identified only the major phases and functions. We wanted to use that representation on the cover of the proposal for greatest effect, but the simplest chart that would meet our minimum requirements for what we felt needed to be identified would not fit on the $8\frac{1}{2} \times 11$-inch cover. And so we created a fold-out cover, as some magazines do today. (As far as we know it was our original idea.) That highly distinctive cover proved to be an excellent attention-getter. The proposal stood out because it was novel. More important, it did something the RFP did not do: It made the requirement and the solution clear. It therefore demanded that the client (meaning anyone on the client's staff) spend at least a few minutes studying the pictorial/functional flowchart on the cover, above which our name (as proposer) was prominently displayed.

Alternative Methods of Flowchart Development

How you go about starting the construction of the flowchart varies according to individual circumstances and your own preferences. You might prefer to make up the lists first and then construct the chart, or you may prefer to do two things concurrently. Either way, there are three general conditions you may encounter:

1. The RFP is so detailed and clear that the chart all but writes itself. You can simply translate the RFP language directly into sequential blocks describing activities and functions, thereby creating your first-draft chart.
2. The RFP is so sketchy and vague that it is difficult to take much more directly from it than the first and last blocks—what you will have to start with and what the client expects you to deliver at the conclusion.
3. An RFP that falls between these extremes—it can be charted with some difficulty and with imaginative input of your own.

There is a significance to these alternative situations. In the first case, a highly detailed RFP that all but dictates the precise solution required may reflect a dogmatic client who will insist on close adherence to the dictates of the RFP, and will reject any proposal that deviates from those dictates. You may be able to judge from the language used in the RFP. The second and third scenarios may indicate that what is presented is all the client knows of its situation and need, or it may be the client is deliberately leaving the door open as an invitation to whatever ideas and suggestions you have to offer. Some RFPs make it clear that such is the case, that your ideas are solicited. Try to determine which is the greatest possibility, as you go about gathering whatever information you can from the preproposal conference, the RFP, and any other sources you can. The better you can "read" the client's attitude, the more likely you are to be the proposer with whom the client feels comfortable. Faced with equally competent competitors, a client would prefer to work with a proposer with whom it feels comfortable.

For the first and third cases, construct a flowchart that describes what the client has portrayed or clearly suggested as the needed program. For the second case, you have a lot of work to do. You will set down whatever you can take directly from the RFP, which may be only the beginning and the end of the chart. You will then have to figure out what is necessary to get from the beginning to the end most efficiently. You may have to do this in progressive stages, starting with a simple chart listing only major phases and functions, and gradually refining and developing it, while being completely responsive to the RFP.

Flowcharts are sequential, revealing or expressing each significant function in terms of phase (time), step-by-step, until the end result is reached. The chart may be at any level. Top management wants to see only the main phases and steps that reveal the logic (rationale) of the system proposed. Lower-level managers want to see more detailed charts, charts that show the implementation—*how* things are done in each phase, charts that demonstrate the feasibility and any claimed advantages of the proposed program. And so you may eventually need to develop more than one chart, some more detailed than the initial one, to implement your presentation strategy. For now, however, we are interested in only the first step, constructing the flowchart that will translate the RFP into a graphic presentation of the program it calls for.

The proper level of detail for this initial or rough-draft flowchart is the level of detail in that RFP. Ideally, the chart will mirror the content of the RFP at the detail of its presentation in the RFP. Add no information, at this point, to what is presented in the RFP. In a few cases, the transfer will be easy, and a logical flowchart will result, but often, you will find that you have a flowchart that leaves a few things to be desired, such as a sensible sequence of events and a complete track of all necessary functions. RFPs often contain undisciplined writing that rambles a bit, is redundant and repetitive, and that contains a few anomalies, contradictions, gaps, or oxymorons. These should be represented in the first draft of the chart, and even highlighted, for that matter. They may be the keys to strategies. That may produce a flowchart that says, in effect, "You can't get there from here."

(You may be strongly tempted here to include that first chart in your proposal to bolster your arguments by showing the client what is wrong and needs correction. Do not do so. A sensitive client may be embarrassed and offended by it. You may refer to problems in your discussion and should do so, but exercise tact. You win more by solving problems than by highlighting them or dwelling on them. You want to convey to the client that you are *willing* to do the necessary work, not that that much work should not *be* necessary.)

As a next step, you must refine the rough-draft chart by straightening out all conflicts of time and function so that you now have a practicable flow represented, one that will get you there from here. By now, you have a pretty good idea of what the project will require, and you have taken the initial steps of designing a program to propose to the client.

In the second case, of the truly vague and uninformative RFP, you may have difficulty gleaning much more than the first "here we are" and last "there is where we want to be" blocks directly from the RFP. It furnishes little help in describing how you are expected to get from here to there. This is ideal for the innovative, inventive proposal writer who is a true expert in the skills and knowledge required for the job. As this expert, imaginative, and resourceful service provider, you map the route yourself, taking what you can get from the RFP and applying your own expertise and imagination to plan the itinerary of the flowchart. Your team, writers, and subject-matter experts working together, do all these things by brainstorming together, under the leadership of the proposal manager. (I led such brainstorming sessions poised before a blackboard, transcribing the team's ideas on the blackboard, developing the draft flowchart there as it was designed by the team. I often used the same method to first develop the checklists as the product of many minds studying the RFP. Today, computer programs may be used for these functions.)

This is an effective strategy for developing the proposal plan and leading the team to devise strategies. When all develop the information together, hammering out agreements in brainstorming sessions, you have the great advantage that all of you have the same understanding on all proposal matters. Communication among team members is greatly improved, of course, and future differences of opinion are minimized. The brainstorming has a synergistic result—the whole is greater than the sum of its parts. A proposal written with an ad hoc team means

- many of the members have had little or no prior experience in writing proposals,
- they are usually working in the pressure cooker of an impossibly short schedule, and
- they must patch together a cohesive whole when the parts may have had divergent ideas.

That initial well-developed flowchart reveals what the RFP says and, more significantly, often indicates what it fails to say and should have said. It also reveals any illogical trends or other weaknesses in the RFP. This knowledge is fodder for the development of successful strategies. Now you are ready to start working seriously on the development of a winning proposal.

Typical Proposal/Contracting Problems

3

Do Clients Always Know What They Want?

Carl Kline provides a program of services to consultants through his San Diego organization, National Referrals, Inc. He recently published in his Internet mailing list an article by Dr. Richard Brakenwagen, Managing Director of Iter International Group of Lincoln, Rhode Island. Carl Kline and Dick Brakenwagen have graciously consented to my use of a portion of the article, which illustrates the major point of some of these introductory pages. The following are Dr. Brakenwagen's words, abstracted from his article:

> While I am in a melancholy mood this morning, I am reflecting on a situation that arises with increasing frequency, where we are asked to provide a proposal from an RFP that clearly indicates that the client doesn't know what his/her problem is! The RFP, is typically couched with "buzz" phrases or words of the time, vague and leave the "expert" with little idea of the client needs related to the hoped for benefit from the consultant.
>
> Typically face-to-face meetings and telephone conversations reveal a middle manager that has been passed the ball

from a senior executive to "get our operations in line in Europe. I'm expecting a 20 percent increase in business in the next two years. Let's get a consultant in here to help us with this." I would be interested in knowing if this sounds familiar to other consultants out there, as we see the incidence of this increasing.

We do have some ideas which we would like to share in this forum that may be of help to others. These ideas fall under the category of "Managing the Client." We have found that in these cases, it is to the client's benefit to do a "due diligence" on the project(s), so as to shape the goals, timetable, and generally establish the expectation for the project. A small fee for this is typically required, however, in this process, all the rocks are turned over and the necessary information is brought forward, which allows us to focus on the real needs of the client. The process also results in our proposal being free of projected cost that is not required. It should also be noted that in 50 percent of these cases, we uncover a need that the client did not recognize, with the result being more business.

The one difficulty in presenting this process to middle management is that he/she is faced with the prospect of going to his/her boss and explaining the need for "establishing the expectation." We have found that positioning ourselves for discussions with the "boss" at this point results in a sigh of relief from the middle manager.

It is our experience that without clearly "establishing the expectation," we are left to submit a proposal that assumes nothing and along with our competition, we submit a proposal that often results in the client suggestion that "this is more than we expected to pay for this work." Often, we refer to our earlier discussion, here, in consideration of the size of the project, spending a small amount of money up front can save a great deal of money in the overall project cost.

Finally, as much as we would like to think the prospective client has read one of the many publications on the subject of choosing and working with consultants, I rarely find that this is the case. I am sure that a good publication can be found in Carl Kline's store (www.4expertise.com/).

My hope is that this article will stimulate some input from other experts, who have other ideas that may be shared and from which we can all benefit.

Dr. Brakenwagen has put a finger neatly on a problem that is even more common than he suggests, and merits the special attention it is to get here. I have posed here the question of whether clients always know what they want.

Defining Terms

I use the term *client* as a generic one as the issuer of an RFP is only a prospective client at this stage. Client refers to the organization to whom a proposal is addressed.

Individuals speaking for an organization with respect to the proposal and procurement are "program managers"—management executives of agencies responsible for carrying out the mission of the agency.

A Request for Proposal or RFP is not a single document normally, but a group of documents often referred to as a "bid set" or "bid package." It usually includes at least these items:

- A letter from the client presenting the general need and articulating the Request for Proposal with a few details, such as type of contract contemplated, schedule dates of events connected with the RFP, and names of relevant officials or executives.
- A Statement of Work, referred to familiarly as the "SOW." This document describes the client's need or problem; what the client requires by way of response, including what must be included in the proposal itself; and any of several other items such as contract details, stipulations, and perhaps some other miscellaneous documents. (For our purposes here, the two main terms, RFP and SOW, are interchangeable, and reference to

either includes both, as appropriate, but for simplicity and consistency, the term RFP will be favored here.)

- In the case of a government agency of some kind, the package also may include literature listing and describing relevant regulations and statutes, and may even include copies of some of those regulations most pertinent to the procurement.
- Drawings and exhibits, as the client deems necessary.

The terms "proposal writer" and "proposer" will be used frequently in these pages. (Government documents often refer to "the proposer.") They may refer to one or more of the individuals actually writing the proposal, but also may be a more general reference to the contractor organization or its management. The context will usually make the reference clear.

The Evolution of a Government RFP

For those not familiar with government contracting, this is probably a good point at which to digress briefly to explain the other side: the government organization and process behind the issuance of a request for proposals.

Executives of an agency decide that they have a need or an obligation to "contract out" certain work to meet certain goals. They develop a document describing the need, what is to be done, and other information necessary to constitute a Statement of Work. They then request the contracting official of their agency to issue a solicitation for proposals. The contracting office is a support service to the program offices of the agency. The program offices are responsible for specifying what is to be done, for providing the funds for the work, and for evaluating the proposals and making choices. The contracting office is responsible for doing all the paperwork (administration) necessary to issue a suitable RFP, soliciting proposals, and ensuring that the procurement is in accordance with relevant laws and regulations and/or company policies.

RFPs are written by fallible humans, often humans who do not write especially well and do not have much of an idea of how to assemble and present a proper RFP. Often, the RFP has been assembled by borrowing an old RFP from another agency or department, and adapting it to the present purpose, with consequent anomalies frequently found.

Such adaptations often do not turn out very well. Sections do not fit together properly. The RFP may be a rambling and completely unclear statement of the client's problem and need. Such shortcomings mean you are trying to hit an ill-defined and moving target!

The SOW is itself often an assembly job, with portions written by different authors and little done to edit and organize the resultant assembly so that a coherent whole emerges. Such weaknesses in creating an RFP are most often the causes of the redundancies, the anomalies, and the contradictions in logic that can appear in RFPs.

There are cases where a client may deliberately not reveal everything about the problem. There are sometimes disagreements within the client organization or other concerns that the client does not wish to reveal, and so the contractor must struggle without having all the relevant information. However, the probability, in most cases, is that the RFP contains all the client knows about the problem and it has no more information to offer.

Another reason some RFPs have relatively little information while others are bursting with detail may result from the client's choice from two schools of thought in writing an RFP. Some clients believe that it is unfair to contractors to withhold any information that would help the contractor write an effective proposal. Other clients operate on the principle that providing too much detail dictates the response and discourages the creative process, when they wish to see all possible ideas offered. They believe that it is in their interest to withhold much of the detail and so encourage innovative solutions.

In time, you may even come to agree with this author that the poorer the quality of the RFP, the better are your chances of winning the contract. That is, the better are your chances if you recognize poor RFPs as the opportunities they so often are *or can be made to be*. Being able to clarify the client's needs according to your own strengths, you can tactfully "rewrite" the RFP so you are the only logical proposer.

Vague or Unclear Writing and Related Problems

Many RFPs and their SOWs suffer from faults ranging from simple lack of detailed clarity to almost total incoherence. They can be so verbose and disorganized in style that they require both translation to simpler language and interpretation of content. They can be vaguely rambling so it is difficult to distinguish a thread or logical flow. They can be so general that convey little information of any use. They can be devoted almost entirely to descriptions of symptoms, rather than identification of problems or causes. They can be totally and obviously inaccurate to a reader who is knowledgeable in the relevant field, describing symptoms or conditions that are illogical and conflicting.

Other RFPs may lack only certain key items of information. They can be clear about the desired outcome or result, but unclear on information you need to design a sensible response to the RFP. Conversely, they may contain a litany of problems but no hint as to what they wish to have done. Some can display more than one of these faults. Such faults may be due to clumsy writing, to the client's uncertainty about the problem and need, or to both conditions.

RFPs can be dogmatic in presenting a description that will brook no independent analysis of the problem or its probable cause. Or they may be equally dogmatic in dictating solutions that appear to you to be obviously impractical or inefficient. To make matters worse, the RFP that mandates a solution by specifying what is to be done also may carry an admonition that nonresponsive proposals will be rejected summarily. "Nonresponsive" means any proposal that offers a plan other than the one suggested in the RFP or deviates in any way from that plan. The client reserves the right to judge this, of course. This can obstruct any effort you might otherwise make to offer the client the best solution.

Those kinds of RFP presentations may thus be reflections of the client's biases, or they may be evidence of attempts to "wire" the procurement for a favored contractor. Where the RFP appears to be deliberately vague so as to favor some chosen supplier, while going through the motions of a fair and open competition, it is likely to discourage many others from even entering the competition. This means an upside of less competition as a partial counter to the downside of a possibly biased client and stacked deck. It often is possible to "unwire" the wired procurement and win the contract despite the difficulty. The fact that the client finds it necessary to wire the procurement suggests the client cannot find justification for a "selected source" or "sole source" procurement, which would be openly directed to the chosen supplier. This, in turn, suggests that unwiring the RFP by presenting an outstanding proposal is possible.

Rather than being wired, it is more likely that the RFP reflects

- narrow thinking by the client,
- a premature RFP (i.e., one issued before the client has a full understanding of the problem and need),
- the client basing suggested approaches or requirements on obsolescent technology, or
- assigning the writing to the least busy person rather than the best qualified person.

Thus, the RFP may not accurately reflect all the relevant information available in the client organization.

A close study of the RFP may reveal one of two causes for the difficulty:

1. Spotty coverage, in which there is clear and accurate definition in some areas and vague rambling in others
2. Spotty coverage where the SOW is clear everywhere except in one critical area

Once you have considered all these factors, you may decide the cost and effort to reply to the RFP is not a good use of your resources and you may make a no-bid decision. Let's assume here that you are going to propose.

Contracting Policies Are a Factor

Federal Acquisition Regulations (FAR) are not so precise and all-encompassing that contracting officials do not have considerable freedom of choice in how they administer their procurements. In fact, it is the very fact that the FAR is voluminous and detailed that permits one to find authorization for almost any choice a contracting official wishes to make. So it is not at all strange that policies and practices in contracting offices vary widely. I have known contracting officers who believed negotiations should be held with the firm submitting the most highly rated technical proposal, while I have also known some who believed the authors of the top three proposals should be invited to negotiate. But I have also known contracting officers who believed everyone who wrote an acceptable proposal should have the opportunity to negotiate.

Another variant in contracting policies that I have encountered is the choice between formal contracting and small purchase procurement methods. Under the Small Purchase Act, a federal agency may award contracts up to $25,000 via a government purchase order—a much simpler way to go. However, while such purchases are *authorized,* they are not *mandated.* The contracting officer may insist on a formal (and much slower) contract negotiation for any procurement in excess of $5,000.

A contracting officer also may choose to survey your working site to confirm its suitability to do the work you have proposed to do. She or he also may wish to examine your accounting records to ensure that your accounting system is satisfactory and/or that you can finance your work (provide operating capital) under the proposed contract. (Advances from the government are possible, but rare.)

In these and many other ways, a contracting officer may exert much or little influence in selecting a proposal for award. Thus, knowing the contracting officer and his or her policies in general is knowledge that may have a great influence on you in developing successful proposal strategies, and it is worthwhile to learn anything you can about this.

Some contracting officers will ask the program executives for their suggestions of potential contractors to receive the RFP, but others firmly reject such suggestions or requests by agency executives. (One such executive with whom I did business had such a contracting officer, and he would call me privately to suggest that I request a copy of the RFP when it was published in the *Commerce Business Daily*, the Department of Commerce's publication that announces contract opportunities and other government-related commercial information.

The evaluation of the technical proposal is normally made by a team, sometimes referred to as a "source selection" board or team. Presumably, the technical evaluation of proposals identifies all those that are acceptable, with the idea of selecting the lowest-priced acceptable proposal for award. A contracting officer may require that if any proposal other than that one is selected for award, the evaluators must write a justification, although this is not usually done. Usually, the selection team will decide which proposal appears to be "in the best interests of the government," which means that lowest price is not always an important criterion, even among a group of proposals that are all deemed acceptable. For example, a proposal scored at 175 points may be chosen over a less expensive one that scored only 160 points because the technical superiority of the first proposal is deemed to be worth the difference in price. However, the point of negotiating with several proposers, and especially asking for a bidder's BAFO (best and final offer), is to arrive at that final determination of value—worth versus cost.

Government versus Private-Sector Proposal Requirements

Federal procurement processes are based on a model code developed some years ago by a special committee of the American Bar Association. State and local governments generally follow the same model, with some significant differences, primarily in the assignment of purchasing authority. Foreign governments who issue RFPs ("tenders") to American suppliers normally follow the practices and procedures recommended here to develop a proposal for American governments. As with any RFP, read and follow the issuer's mandates.

In some cases in the private sector, especially those in which government prime contractors issue their own contracts and subcontracts, procurement methods also are based on that model. (In fact, government contracts sometimes require specifically that subcontracts be procured competitively.) However, most private-sector procurement calls for much simpler proposals than government. For one thing, in the private sector, there exists the tendency to assume that you are qualified to be engaged in whatever business or career you identify as your own. For example, in the private sector, it is assumed that someone offering an engineering service is a qualified engineer, although the engineer certainly is entitled to and should offer his or her bona fides and any evidence possible attesting to his or her excellence and achievements. The government will want proof that you are a qualified engineer, before considering how good an engineer you are.

The differences between the requirements of the private sector and the government sector do not invalidate the concepts presented here in their applicability to the private sector. Those approaches to proposal writing are equally effective when competing for business via simpler proposals called for in the private sector, although the proposals themselves may not require all the information and formalities the government agencies call for when they request proposals. Even in the case of government procurement, however, where a contract is relatively small and does not justify a full-blown proposal, an informal letter proposal of a few pages may be used. All the principles of good proposal writing practice apply in either case.

Common, Uncommon, and Special Problems

There are several different types of problems normally encountered in responding to an RFP, in addition to those enumerated in the previous chapter. Many are routine problems inherent in the procurement process, especially that of a large bureaucracy, and you may expect to encounter problems of this type more or less regularly. For example, most contractors find there is never enough time to write the best possible proposal, even when one has received a draft RFP as much as a year in advance. (The final RFP may include quite different requirements than those contemplated in the draft RFP, so serious proposal writing cannot really begin until the final RFP arrives.) One never has exactly the right people on staff or, even if the right people are on staff, they often are not available to be assigned to staff the project proposed or even to work on the proposal. Likewise, one never has enough senior people available to assign to the proposal writing, and must use second-tier people. One never has the exactly right, idealized qualifications called for by the RFP, so one must judge how close to those ideals one must come to qualify. You can count on conditions such as these cropping up as complications in carrying out the average proposal effort.

The good news is that, ironically, we appeared to enjoy much greater success with those proposals prepared on the shortest and most difficult schedule. Because such schedules never gave us time to have second thoughts and revise or rewrite, we were forced to get it right the first time!

There are special problems peculiar to certain types of procurements and to the proposals required to win the hearts and signatures of those clients. There is, for example, the contract for close-in support work that the client feels requires a contractor with facilities that are physically nearby. There is the project that is to be conducted at some location distant from you so you must recruit and train staff in that location. There is the project that requires you to propose a site for which you can guarantee availability, even though you have no guarantee of a contract as yet. There is the RFP that requires you to have guaranteed recourse to facilities that are not under your control. There is the RFP that calls on you to guarantee during the life of the contract the availability of highly specialized experts at any time. And there is the often-used requirement that you guarantee the availability of all those senior project staff whose résumés you proposed or equivalently qualified substitutes, even if the award is made and the project starts as much as a year after you submitted your proposal. Many of these guarantees are made by a proposer with fingers crossed and a faith that a means will be found for crossing that river when the time comes.

Then there are the very special problems that are peculiar to an individual requirement and usually result from special stipulations or restrictions imposed by the RFP for one reason or another. And finally there are the special problems that arise because of special or unusual circumstances of the requirement, such as an unusual problem or extraordinary need of the client. Some of these problems are minor impediments and can be solved almost routinely, but some are major obstacles that must be overcome through special measures and a great deal of ingenuity and resourcefulness. Some of these problems are, in fact, so serious and so difficult to overcome that entire chapters are devoted here to discussing them and suggesting strategies for coping successfully with them.

For example, the EPA required a formidable array of engineers, physicists, chemists, and other professionals to be available for consulting assignments, as a condition of one large contract. The successful proposer expended a great deal of time and effort entering into agreements with a number of local universities and several subcontractors to satisfy this requirement.

Problems Are Often Opportunities

You may or may not agree that problems are opportunities. However, there is no doubt that at least some problems are or can be the launch pad for the creation of special opportunities. Special proposal problems can be unique, never encountered before, rare but not unknown, or even common and encountered frequently in some form. They may arise from any area or element of the RFP. One problem that is not uncommon, for example, is the mandate that the number of pages of your proposal be limited to some given number. That limitation may appear to you to be too restrictive to allow you to make what you deem to be a necessary and proper presentation, which makes it a problem indeed. Another problem may be the imposition of unreasonably demanding, even special and rare demands for credentials that you must present to be considered qualified as a contractor for the work to be done. Another is an unreasonable schedule for production of the proposal, such as a due date so closely following the date on which the RFP became available that it is virtually impossible to produce a sensible proposal in time to meet the deadline. Still another is a declaration that only responsive proposals will be accepted (those that follow the RFP exactly) and alternative proposals will be summarily rejected (even if they offer innovative, faster, or less expensive problem solving). The client assumes the right to be the sole authority in determining what is and what is not responsive.

Try to determine if there is some reason for the special condition (although the true reason may not be at all logical). This knowledge may help you identify a USP for your proposal. With enough imagination and resourcefulness, you may turn that lemon into lemonade. In fact, finding any item that appears to be beyond the norm or other than a practice to be normally expected should alert you to the possibility that it may be a seed bed for the development of special strategies. Necessity may drive you to develop an innovation you would otherwise not have conceived, proving the cliché that necessity is the mother of invention.

A General Approach

All problems can be solved. In fact, as suggested above, these problems are themselves often the keys to success for at least these reasons:

- They are problems your competitors face too. The more difficult the problems are, the better it can be for you, if you are a hard-working strategist. The more difficult the problems are, the more discouraging they are to your competitors, more of whom will drop out, deciding that competing in this case is not worth the trouble of trying to overcome the difficulties or the possibility that they may not succeed in overcoming them. Fewer competitors means a higher probability of your success.
- The more imaginative you are at using this challenge as an inspiration for a winning strategy, the better are your chances for outclassing all competition and winning the contract. Your general qualifications are always an important factor, but an

imaginative approach in overcoming difficulties always has a great appeal and can be the decisive element. An RFP that presents special problems is a goad that inspires the hard-working strategist to develop new ideas.

There are thus three factors here that you ought to consider as operating principles:

1. Recognize and welcome the problem-ridden RFP as a special opportunity to use your imagination and develop winning new ideas.
2. Scour and absorb the RFP—don't just read it—for worry items and other seeds to the development of devastatingly effective strategies. Scouring means finding and digesting both overt and covert information, appreciating nuances and connotations. It means multiple readings, weighing every word, reading between the lines, checking references and citations, and developing critical-item lists and flowcharts.
3. Identify some factor that you believe is important enough to the client to influence the client's final decision. Develop this as a main or capture strategy, and build your proposal on it. Make your main strategy drive the proposal by integrating that strategy throughout all elements of your proposal.

4

RFP Strategies

Reading versus Searching the RFP

Reading an RFP, even many, many times, is one thing; *searching* it, searching for the keys to success, is quite another and is what you should be doing. You should be searching for worry items, especially, but also for weaknesses in the client's descriptions and suggestions, for pitfalls to avoid, and for clues to developing a main USP for this proposal. You are searching for the key(s) to a winning *strategy*. Those keys may be in the RFP. They also may be in your own head, triggered by the prompts found in the RFP. You may find valuable clues between the lines, or the most obscure note may provoke an important idea. (In at least one case, I found the clue leading to success in a section of the RFP that defined terms used in the RFP because one of the definitions was contrary to usual standards and offered us a great cost advantage.)

The activity should continue to the point where you are getting no new information or ideas in your understanding of the need and of the client's position. Only then have you studied the RFP enough. The search is not entirely aimed at uncovering information that must be inferred. It is also a means for stimulating your own thought processes, a kind of solo brainstorming where you play all the roles of several participants, a form of incubation.

RFP Study as Incubation

That relentless attack on the RFP—the scouring for clues—is, in fact, an incubation, as explained in Chapter 1, discussing the origins of inspiration and invention. The intense and prolonged effort solicits the help of your subconscious. You may get insights and ideas directly while doing this study. It is more likely that the best ideas will come to you spontaneously later while doing something entirely unrelated to the project. Incubation works only when you have carried out a maximum conscious search, feeding information to your subconscious.

Other Aids to Finding the Keys

There are other techniques that will help you visualize the project, incubate the messages, and develop special insights. In conjunction with reading and searching the RFP, try using the following two steps:

1. Prepare a list of requirements. It should actually be two or three lists, as follows (also see page 26):
   - Those items of information that must be presented in the proposal. Glean them carefully and completely from the RFP.
   - Those items and/or characteristics that must be included in the project or work plan proposed. Carefully glean those too from the RFP.
   - The proposal evaluation criteria, described in or inferred from the RFP.
2. Prepare a flowchart from the SOW (see page 29), presenting the program as described in the RFP. If there is sufficient detail provided there, present a complete program. If there is not enough clear detail in the Statement of Work to chart a complete program, develop the flowchart as far as you can and add any missing elements from your own knowledge and initiative to portray the program you infer the RFP describes to satisfy the client's need. On the chart, mark which elements are taken from the RFP

and which are your creations. You will use this information to argue your case.

Go over the RFP again and again, in rough draft, upgrading, revising, and refining, until you are confident that your lists and flowchart are an accurate and complete representation of the RFP and what you believe is a logical presentation of what the RFP presents or implies, without passing judgment on it yet. Then you may examine the chart for practicality, problems inherent in it as presented, and/or better ways to do the job.

First, check your chart for completeness and logical integrity. Starting with the first block, ask "why?" The information in the next block should answer this question. Continue in the same way to the last block. Starting with the last block, ask "how?" The information in the preceding block should answer this question. Continue in the same way to the first block. Suppose, for example, you plan a trip, and the first three blocks say, CARRY A MAP, FIND THE ROUTE, and REACH DESTINATION. Using the above two tests, you will see how they validate your chart. If any block fails the why/how test, something is missing, misstated, or out of sequence. You may decide the level of detail to use in describing the functions and actions—the test will work at any level of complexity.

You may wish to present this chart to the client as a representation of what the RFP states. If a chart offers a different tack from what the client thought the RFP stated, this may be the clue to a successful win strategy. Certainly, it will support your arguments for whatever alternatives you present to the client as you work out your own program. Between the flowchart and the checklists, you can find the keys you need to identify or develop worry items and strategies.

The Client Who Knows It All

Most of the foregoing discussions were inspired by experience with RFPs that reflected a client's uncertainty or lack of clear understanding of his or her own needs. One may encounter another kind of case: the client who knows or believes he or she knows exactly what the problem and proper cure are, and mandates the required program. This can be a most difficult problem to deal with, both when the client's mandated program is a good one and when it happens that the mandated program is, in your opinion, all wrong and will not produce the best results!

In the first case, when the client is right about the logical solution and directs proposers to propose their own versions of projects that will implement that solution, you have a marketing problem. By compelling all respondents to the RFP to present an implementation of the same general solution to the problem, the client has (1) narrowed the opportunities for identifying competitive strategies and (2) encouraged maximum participation by making responding to the RFP so easy.

On the other hand, you still may search for a worry item on which to hang a strategy. You also may still pursue imaginative ideas for implementing the client's idea of what is needed. Let us suppose, for example, that the client has a software program that must run every week, but it takes far too much time to run because it was originally written in haste and without regard to relative efficiency. Now the client wants the program updated to make it more efficient and run much faster. The client even may have stipulated that run time must be reduced by at least 50 percent.

The challenge is now a technical one. Typically, software efficiency is in inverse proportion to cost, and cost is in direct proportion to development time and labor. So there are three parameters to balance: run time, schedule time, and cost. The client in our hypothetical case has provided the minimum goal of run time and provided a schedule, so the chief factor you have to work with is cost.

You can set one of two limits:

1. Determine the lowest cost to achieve 50 percent reduction in run time within the schedule.
2. Determine the cost of achieving the lowest possible run time within the schedule.

You must now decide what to trade off. Here, you must judge what is the most important consideration to the client, run time reduction or cost? Is either a worry item? Or is meeting the schedule—that is, achieving the objective within the schedule—a worry item? In other words, what is the client's symbol of greatest success, keeping the cost down or maximizing the improvement? So, even with a mandated solution and only relatively minor technical problems to solve, strategy is not only possible, but will probably be decisive.

Even more difficult is the situation of the RFP in which the client mandates the solution, or at least the approach, but you judge the approach or solution to be all wrong. It is obviously not even close to the best possible solution, and your professional pride alone will stand in the way of your agreeing to undertake the program on that basis. But the client makes it clear that only "responsive" proposals will be considered. This is normally taken to mean only proposals that implement the suggested program.

It seems rather difficult, on the face of it, to find an opportunity in this problem. This may very well be a situation in which the client is setting up an obstacle course for everyone but a favored contractor, who is the only one the client will find to be responsive. You are faced with what appears to be a no-win situation. You either agree to undertake a program that is all wrong when you know a much better way to proceed, or you propose the better way knowing that by so doing you are probably going to have your proposal disqualified as nonresponsive and suffering a loss of time and money in what seems to be a futile effort. Rather than opportunity, you are faced with a number of choices, none of which is very appealing:

1. You file a letter with the client, arguing for an amendment to the RFP.
2. You no-bid the RFP with a lengthy letter detailing your reasons.
3. You go along with the plan of the RFP, offering a responsive proposal, but offering an argument for an alternative, which you also propose.
4. You submit the proposal you think to be the right one, arguing your case.

5. You go along with the RFP, hoping to win and planning to persuade the client to change plans after award.

Your Right to Protest

There is a sixth possibility. If the client is a federal government agency, you have the right to protest an administrative, not legal, procedure, although protests are reviewed by a staff of lawyers at the Government Accounting Office (GAO). You may protest at any time, even after you have opted for any of the other choices and found that they did not produce the desired results. You need only file a letter with either the client or the GAO, explaining what you think is illegal or inequitable.

While most contractors who file protests do so after they have learned they are not the winners—that is, after an award has been announced—it is not necessary to wait. You may protest a procurement at any point in the process, even to protest the RFP or the announcement of a procurement to be made. Apparently this right is not well known: most contractors appear to believe they must wait until an award is announced.

The advantage to protesting at this early stage of the procurement is that if you are successful in your arguments, you can force an amendment to the RFP, correcting the condition that is the basis of your protest. However, a successful protest may have another result: it may cause a complete cancellation of the procurement. And at best, it confers the benefits, if any, on your competitors too, so your gain, if any, is questionable.

In fact, there is probably no best strategic choice for all such situations. What is the most successful strategy varies with the individual circumstances of the given case. However, in actual experience with this kind of proposal situation, I have found that a strategy based on choice number 3 or 4 has usually been the most effective one. The third choice does furnish a responsive proposal, while it also argues for a better choice and provides an alternative proposal for that choice. The fourth choice may work as well or even better because it is a more emphatic declaration. Handled properly, both choices 3 and 4 provide grounds for a future protest if your proposal is not taken seriously by the client or you are declared to be unresponsive and so disqualified. That choice may very well turn a lemon into lemonade, a problem birthing an opportunity.

With either 3 or 4 as your choice of strategy, you may make the argument in your proposal that you propose a better way of achieving the result called for, even if different from that suggested in the RFP, and therefore your proposal is a responsive one. If your argument is strong enough, the client will sense that you will not submit quietly to a summary dismissal as "nonresponsive." You do have a good argument to present in a protest: Because you are an independent contractor and not an employee of the government, the government does not have the right to tell you how to get a job done, but only to tell you what result is needed. It is up to you to propose what you believe to be the best way to achieve this result. Therefore, you believe your proposal is, indeed, responsive.

This approach has worked well in a number of cases. For maximum effectiveness, it is important to have decided in advance that this will be the approach, however, so that the proposal is structured overall to support this strategy. Early in the proposal you should set the theme of addressing results, not methods. It should be addressed in the statement in which the proposer demonstrates an understanding of the requirement, focusing on the achievement of the client's desired result. This theme should then be maintained through flowchart analyses and all other aspects of the proposal so there can be no doubt that the proposal does address the client's need, which is a certain outcome or result, and not a method of achieving that outcome.

It is wise to minimize and, if possible, completely avoid any attack on or sharp criticism of the approach stipulated by the RFP. Treat it as one way to do the job, but you know of a better way. Do not assume that the client is truly married to all the ideas expressed in the RFP. That is, there may have been no special purpose to the client's stipulation of method or plan. Clients who do not do purchasing often probably do not have an RFP format of their own, and often such a client simply borrows a sample RFP from another agency, innocently following its language without critical evaluation of how well the model fits the need. In fact, your proposal may come to the client as a great enlightenment of the advantages of keeping the doors open to all ideas and inviting them from proposers. It is therefore far wiser for you to proceed on the basis of this assumption and write approvingly of or without direct comment on the suggested program, going on then to the better way you wish to propose. Focus your arguments positively instead of negatively by stressing the advantages of what you propose, with minimal criticism—perhaps even minimal mention or citation—of the design ideas in the RFP.

The Risks of Persuasiveness

There is some risk in being persuasive in a case such as this. In any procurement where you somehow convince the client that the RFP was defective and presented a faulty plan or was based on a false premise, the client may feel compelled to take some drastic action to correct the original fault. That action may be an amendment to the RFP, issued to all who requested a copy of the RFP originally, with an appropriate extension of the due date for proposal submissions, or it may be a cancellation of the RFP, which may or may not be reissued in a corrected version later. The client may be inspired by a sense of fair play, trying to level the playing field for all competitors, although that may seem unfair to you as the discoverer of the faults. But it may be inspired by a fear that one or more of the competitors who did not succeed in winning the contract will lodge protests with the GAO. There are contractors who protest nearly every award for which they competed unsuccessfully because it is an informal process that requires only a simple letter setting forth the facts and the grounds for the protest.

The Protest Process

A protest may be filed directly with the GAO or with the contracting official, who must then forward your protest to the GAO. It is an administrative process, not a legal one, and to file your protest you need only state the facts as you see them in a simple letter to the head of GAO, the Comptroller General. You do not need a lawyer, although some who protest do retain a lawyer, which may be a mistake, complicating a simple process that is not legal. GAO will require the contracting officer to respond to them with an official version of the facts, and you will get a chance to review it and respond to it, after which GAO will make a decision. (In practice, there may be multiple exchanges of facts and opinions.)

One contracting officer who appeared as a speaker at a proposal seminar said that while he hated getting protests of an award because they always caused him so much extra work, he approved of and even applauded my recommendation to use the protest when one thinks it justified. He approved the use of the protest in general, as an appeal contractors have to counter faults and illegalities in procurement. Presumably contracting officials will do what they can to avoid creating a basis for protests.

Proposers often raise questions, requests, or objections, such as asking for an extension of the schedule or some other change in the RFP. The result is unpredictable. The client simply refuses to take any action or, fearing a protest, may make an appropriate change. But the client's reaction to a protest is also unpredictable and may range from agreeing with the protestor and making appropriate changes to fighting the protest or even cancelling the procurement, if the project is of no urgency. This is not an uncommon outcome, so a protest "victory" can end up being a hollow one. It is often the possibility of a protest, especially one that the GAO is likely to agree with, that influences the client's willingness to make changes.

This is a risk for the client and the contracting official, the risk of serious interference with implementation of the contract and a great deal of extra work for the client and contracting officer. But it is also a risk for the proposer. Should a client be persuaded by your arguments and therefore award you the contract despite that action representing at least a partial reversal or nullification of the original terms of the RFP, chances are one or more of the other contenders for the contract will protest. That protest may or may not affect you and the award. Even if the GAO should uphold such a protest, the client may not be compelled to cancel the procurement, but may continue with the award as being "in the best interests of the government." There is ample precedent for this. As a practical matter, a protest generally delays the start of a project until the issue is resolved or the project cancelled.

There is another side to this question of the benefits of a protest. On one occasion, I was retained by a quite prominent corporation that had never pursued government contracts before. I was to write a proposal for them, from which they did not expect a successful outcome. Of course, I felt compelled to ask why, if they did not expect to win, did they wish to write a proposal?

The answer was that they wanted to get into the game—government contracting, that is—and thought this good for government agencies to recognize them as a serious candidate for government work. There was a well-known competitor whom they were sure would underprice them with a less sophisticated product and win the contract.

Thus armed in advance with the expectation of not winning, I advised studying the RFP carefully to see whether we could somehow find something on which to base a protest later. My client agreed and we set about making the search, found what we thought would serve the purpose, and proceeded to write the proposal in such a way as to prepare the groundwork for a protest.

All went as predicted, and notice that the award was to be made to the competitor was issued. We filed our protest promptly. The result was that our protest was upheld as being based on valid ground, the notice of award was rescinded, and the procurement was cancelled. My client was pleased, to my surprise. He thought that denying the contract to his competitor was almost as good as winning, especially after he visited the agency to discuss the project and emerged with some other business he was able to get on a selected-source basis!

When a Protest Fails

The formal protest is not the only option a contractor has. Since the protest is an administrative process, there is nothing to prevent a contractor whose protest has not succeeded from going to court with a formal lawsuit. Regulations do not require that an award or the start of a program be halted when a protest is made, but it is the usual option of the agency to do so, perhaps in consideration of other possible action by the protesting contractor, such as a lawsuit. The history of such cases is not encouraging for contractors, especially when the contractor did not file a protest and a subsequent lawsuit until after the contract was awarded. Even worse, for the contractor's chance of success, is the case where the lawsuit did not get into court until the project had been launched. There is a reluctance to set aside a contract that has been awarded, although it has been done, and an even greater reluctance to call a halt to a project that has been started.

It happens in such cases that often the court finds the plaintiff made his or her case, but it is not in the government's best interest to halt the project and hold a new competition. It would cost the government a great deal of money and delay an important work. Therefore, the court can only regretfully inform the plaintiff that, as a practical matter, he was close but no cigar.

One conclusion to draw from this is that it is usually a mistake to wait until the award has been announced to lodge a protest. If you see something about a procurement that you believe is wrong at some earlier point in the process, and you believe it is in your interest to solicit corrective action, the time to protest is immediately. A client of mine called me on one occasion to complain that he had received an RFP that called for proposals to be delivered three days later, and the contracting officer refused his request to extend the date. I advised my client to send the contracting officer a letter plainly identifying itself as a protest. He did so, and the deadline for submittal of proposals was promptly extended. It would have done him no good to scrawl a hasty proposal and protest later that there had not been time to write a proper proposal.

Be aware of your right to protest, when, and how. Then evaluate whether this is a good or bad move for you in that particular case.

Gathering Intelligence

The Key to Strategy Development

Marketing is inevitably competitive—as competitive, in its own way, as war, because you are pitted against others who are fighting to win those same customers and dollars you are pursuing. Your marketing strategy thus must focus on combating and overcoming competition as well as on persuading prospects of the value of what you offer. You depend on information—marketing intelligence—to inspire and develop your winning strategies. The power of your strategies is thus heavily dependent on the quality of your information—the accuracy, appropriateness, and completeness of the marketing intelligence you gather.

The Focus of Intelligence Gathering

The two major objectives of your marketing are:

1. Persuading a client to want and buy what you offer
2. Satisfying that want by buying from you, rather than from one of your competitors

Depending on how you evaluate your marketing problems and opportunities in the given case, your strategy may be to focus especially on one or the other of these objectives, but in some situations you may wish to place equal emphasis on both objectives.

Your competition is not necessarily restricted to other contractors vying to win a proposal contest, but may include the client's own idea of the proper solution. Some RFPs do include that as a problem, when the client expresses a strong affection for a given solution that you find to be all wrong. In such case, you may find it necessary to take issue with major provisions of the RFP, and compete as best you can with the client's own notions of what is needed. (See Chapter 4 for more about this problem.)

We usually operate on certain starting premises and then adjust these premises to the facts at hand as we perceive and interpret those facts. Presumably in a typical proposal situation the client has already felt a want for and decided to buy the service or product that is the subject of the RFP. So the client does not have to be induced to feel a want. But is that really the case?

What is undecided and yet to be contested is the identity of the proposer and proposed solution that the client judges to best satisfy the want. The RFP has been issued to others, of course, so one view of your major objective is that it is to outsell your competitors rather than to induce a sense of want. You must induce the client to feel a greater want for your proposed program than for that of any other programs. The service or product you will offer the client in your proposal will differ from ones your competitors offer. You must *sell* what you propose. What you propose must be made more attractive than what your competitor proposes. And to do that effectively, you need to have an idea what your competitor will propose. This effort, to get a good idea what your competitors will propose, is the purpose of your intelligence efforts (just like any spying effort).

Intelligence Needs

The first line of attack in gathering intelligence is the information supplied directly by the client in the RFP, and in any preproposal conference or subsequent amendments or modifications to the original RFP and, in some cases, what you already know about the client from prior experience or from the grapevine. The abundance and quality of information available from these initial sources determine, or at least suggest, how much more information there is to be gained from other sources. As an experienced marketer, you will usually get a sense of whether you have or are missing relevant information. Still, you will probably make a check to see if there is more useful information available before you decide on how extensive a search you will make for more data.

In some cases, you start out knowing in advance at least some information or what kind of information you need. If the contract will require hiring some class of labor you have not hired before or hiring people in some other part of the country, you know that you will have to ascertain the available supply of such labor where you need it and what you will have to pay for it. You need to know if the contract is currently in force for a continuing project and is now up for renewal and required by law or policy to be rebid. In that case, you will want to find out what the client has been paying the current contractor. If the contract has been in force for a long time and other contractors have held it in the past, you want as complete and as detailed a history of the program as possible. You may want to know also which other contractors were invited to submit proposals. You will want to know as much as possible about your competitors and what they are likely to offer. By now, your intelligence gathering is beginning to develop sharply defined objectives.

For example, take the typical "laundry list" contract a government agency may award and maintain permanently for a range of editorial services—writing, editing, proofreading, illustration, and photography. Such a contract is usually for two or three years and must be placed for open competition each time the end of its term approaches. You have a right to know what the client has been paying for each service and to which contractors, although you should be interested only in the current contractor and the length of the contract. If that contractor has been successful for many years in winning the award each time it has come up for renewal, that is important intelligence. It means they will probably be difficult to dislodge. You will want to find out why they have been successful in winning the contract each time it comes up for renewal. Seek answers to the following questions: Is there a special key to winning this contract? Have protests been filed by other contenders for the contract? Does the contractor have a special reputation you should know about?

As long as your search for intelligence creates as many new questions as answers, your search for information is not complete.

In many cases, you will have been given what purports or appears to be complete information as the RFP and, possibly, in a preproposal conference. On closer examination, it appears to be far too little, too general, or too vague to help you write a focused proposal. Your search goal is to know at least as much about the RFP requirements as the client and competitors put together.

A general truth in intelligence gathering is that you will use only a fraction of what you gather. Nevertheless, you must gather all the information available and study it to decide what will be most useful. It may be only 10 percent of what you have accumulated, but you want to be sure that it is the critical 10 percent, the most important elements of your research. You can determine what is best only by gathering and examining it all. You do not stop until you can find nothing more that is relevant.

A Few Targets of Intelligence Gathering

You should have an intelligence plan and be seeking specific kinds of information. At the same time, you must be alert and watchful for useful information that comes unanticipated, a fortunate surprise. *Serendipity* is the word for that, and it does not happen to you unless yours is a prepared mind, ready to recognize and welcome a fortuitous discovery that may not fit neatly into an existing category in your intelligence plan. When this valuable information that you did not know you were looking for drops into your lap, be ready to capture and use it. That fortunate windfall aside, however, following are a few ideas of specific kinds and classes of information you might wish to target in pursuing marketing intelligence:

- One or more of the client's worry items, or keys to finding them.
- Answers to questions you would like to have been able to ask the client privately. (An excellent preparatory step for this is to draw up a set of questions you would have asked, and make them specific objectives of your intelligence search.)
- The history behind the development of the requirement or other information connected with it in any way, such as earlier contracts or projects on which the current RFP was based.
- Prior contracts awarded by the client that appear to be related to or of similar nature.
- Information relative to any apparent gap in the information offered in the RFP.
- Any information that you think ought logically to have been in the RFP but wasn't. (Again, it is most useful to have prepared a written list of these items.)
- Information that you believe the client deliberately withheld from the RFP. (This is often not apparent, but sometimes it is glaringly evident to the experienced marketer.)
- Guides for pricing—that is, intimations of the client's probable budget.
- Identities of competitors.
- Competitors' products and contracting histories.
- Any and all relevant information of any kind, even if you do not know where it fits at first and can be labeled only "miscellaneous."

Let's look just a bit more closely at some of these information items and the related areas of concern.

Worry Items

"Good" worry items are a major find in providing opportunities for powerful win strategies. "Good" refers to an important issue for the client and how worried the client is or can be persuaded to be over the item.

Discovering a client's chief concern is always an excellent candidate to become the key to a successful win strategy. (Addressing minor worries will not win the contract for you.)

If, for example, the RFP lays great stress on the absolute need for the schedule dates to be unchanging deadlines, it becomes clear that the client has some reason to be especially concerned about the schedule. That is a worry item, but it is not enough. What would be the terrible consequences for the client if the schedule were not kept? *That* is probably the real worry item.

On the other hand, how serious is that worry item in the client's mind? Suppose the client is a worrier by nature, and always reveals a half-dozen or more worries. Solving which worry or set of worries will motivate the client's decision to hire you? Identify and respond to all worries, but prioritize.

On the other hand, it may be that as far as you can determine, the client has no major worries about the procurement, other than the normal concerns of staying within the budget, finding a dependable contractor, managing a smooth-running and successful project, and achieving the goals of the procurement. Rather than the client having no special concerns about the project, it is more likely the client is an unusually calm and confident individual or simply does not want any worries to show. In any case, given an apparent lack of special concerns, you may consider directing the search in the direction of finding good ideas for *giving* the client a worry item or two—finding items about which the client ought to be worried, and working those into effective arguments as worry items upon which you may base strategies. See if you can discover what would be the consequence for the client of failing to deliver everything on schedule. What if you could meet the client's technical specifications, but know that they will fall short of completely solving the problem addressed by the RFP?

Where you can create an effective worry item that is not even hinted at in the RFP, it is likely to prove to be an excellent competitive strategy. If you uncover a worry item that no competitor mentions, it says something for you and your work as surpassing that of your competitors' work. Further, you have solved a problem that no others have because they did not know they were supposed to. It would almost be like having the only complete RFP!

Information on the Background of the Procurement

Any information underlying the development of the RFP can be of supreme importance. Such information may itself be the key to the most important worry item, but whatever the case, it always helps greatly to know the background of the procurement, such as chronic problems the client has had but perhaps does not wish to disclose in the RFP or thought were in no way related to the current procurement need. There may have been an earlier procurement and contract that failed to solve the problem, for example. In such case, the product of the earlier procurement may have been discarded so that this is to be an entirely new and separate effort to solve the problem. Or the product may be in use, but functioning poorly. It is not unusual for clients to contract for services to troubleshoot and retrofit a "fix" to a product or system. It helps greatly to know whether this is such a case.

A change of management may be responsible for the RFP. New management may so dislike an existing system, or the approach taken in designing that system (perhaps without a sound argument for antipathy to it), that the new procurement is to replace the existing system as quietly as possible. And where a procurement is to recompete an existing term contract because it is routinely required, it helps greatly to get a sound indication of whether the client prefers to keep the incumbent contractor, wants to change contractors, or does not care one way or the other. Of course, if you find a reason to believe that the client is definitely interested in changing contractors, it is a great help to get some idea of why the client wants change.

One thing to be watchful for in trying to uncover information about the history of a project is any record of earlier procurements of relevant studies the client may have contracted for. In many cases, a client will have contracted for one or more studies to gather information necessary to develop a budget and write an RFP. A careful study of prior awards by the client may uncover information of this kind. There may be a pattern disclosed or at least suggested by the stream of procurements. That can give you valuable insights into possible worry items and may provide excellent clues to several items. It can help you in a number of ways, such as

- estimating the client's budget,
- perceiving the client's long-range goals,
- understanding the client's normal practices in procurement, and
- learning the client's preferences and tendencies in making awards.

What you believe ought logically to have been in the RFP may have been withheld through oversight, but it may also be that the client deliberately withheld certain information for any of many reasons. The client's logic may be quite different from yours, of course. Key information may be deliberately withheld for the client's own political reasons or because the client wisely wants to encourage wide-ranging and independent thinking by proposers, as mentioned earlier (see Chapter 3) to encourage the submission of as many free-ranging ideas as possible. A client may thus have deliberately kept the SOW unspecific. In any case, such an RFP is your license to suggest innovative solutions and alternative proposals.

Cost Information

The client normally withholds information that would reveal the budget for the procurement—the client's own estimate of what the project should cost as a maximum. In fact, in government procurement, the client must keep such information out of the RFP, although occasionally the client consciously or unconsciously gives very broad hints of the budget by revealing such items as the client's own estimate of professional work hours of effort required, or even mentions a dollar figure. Normally, overt clues are absent from the RFP, and you must use your own experience, instincts, and related expertise to try to read between the lines and estimate the client's budget, aided by whatever data you can gather in your research.

Availability of Funds

In some cases, the client expects to get but does not yet have budget approval or funds allocated for the procurement. Somewhere in the RFP, this will be revealed with something such as "Funds are not yet available for this procurement." How you react to such a notification in the RFP is up to you. Some contractors make it a flat policy that they never respond to an RFP that bears such a statement. (I have personally "won" contracts that were never funded, so there was no benefit in winning and I lost time and money.) This is the risk you accept when you decide to submit a proposal without assurance that it is funded. The pros of pursuing such a project are primarily that there are others who definitely will not respond to the RFP, so your competition will be greatly lessened. The cons are, of course, principally the hazard of winning the project but never getting a contract for it. You will have to weigh that possibility against the cost of preparing a proposal.

Responsibility for Costs

In government procurement, the RFP normally requires that the costs be submitted in a separate document, a cost proposal. (The main proposal is known as the technical proposal, and in some cases—where management of the program is considered to be a major undertaking— there may be a management proposal, too.) The client then separates the cost proposal so that those who review and evaluate the technical proposal do not know the costs, and make their decisions and recommendations based on the perceived merits of the technical proposal, not on costs.

Other proposal-writing organizations also isolate costs from their technical proposal because they see no reason for those writing the technical proposal to be concerned with dollars and cents. So perhaps it is not surprising that the writers of the technical proposal tend to shrug off any responsibility for the cost of the proposed project, saying that costing is not their concern but that of their comptroller. This is not a logical position, of course. Those who design the program proposed are inevitably responsible for the amount that appears on the bottom line of the cost estimate submitted to the client.

The accountants do not really cost the proposal; they only develop the numbers by translating the proposal writers' stipulated labor and other cost items into dollars, and add the organization's profit. Often enough, at this point, the proposal writers complain about the end price, blaming the accountants for what they believe to be too high a bid to win, still disclaiming any responsibility for the end cost. To combat this effectively, it is essential that the designers of the proposed program have some clear idea of what the not-to-exceed end cost must be, and they must understand approximately what their design will cost the client. It is a mistake to insulate the proposal writers from the cost information. The opposite tack should be taken of programming positive steps into the proposal process—that is, educating the proposal writers in a few basics of pricing—to make sure that the writers understand all the cost consequences of their design choices. Moreover, this should be done early enough in the proposal development so that there is time and opportunity to make adjustments before the program design is firmed up.

This is not to say that your proposal must come in as the lowest priced one. Far from it, having too low a price (which can be interpreted as not understanding the need) can be as deadly a thrust to its chances as too high a price can be. The client will try to negotiate with the contractor submitting the best proposal if the cost specified is within reasonable range of the client's budget. But if the proposed effort imposes a cost that is so far out of the ballpark of the client's budget that there is little hope of being able to reach an accommodation through negotiation, that will usually be the end of it: The client usually will not attempt a negotiation. Thus, intelligence as to the client's ideas of what the project should cost and has budgeted for the job can be critically important as a rein on the designers' ideas and to not underbid when funds are available.

Methods for research are many. Some are classic, others innovative or contrived. One method, perhaps the main and most traditional one, is by searching existing documents.

Research into Relevant Documents

Under federal law (the Freedom of Information Act, especially), you have the right to see or demand copies of public documents. This includes the contracts of incumbent contractors. You do not have the right to see proprietary and/or confidential information of the incumbent contractor, such as their internal cost factors, or processes, methods, and records. Therefore, the government will excise certain data from any copies they supply to you.

Reviewing and studying government records of relevant procurement history are one way to develop a reasonable estimate. But you need not necessarily rely on records in government offices for such information. Sometimes there are unacceptably lengthy delays in getting information under the Freedom of Information Act, so the information is not available in time to be helpful to you. However, if you or your library has *Commerce Business Daily* data on file (especially in computer files, with a search engine to help you find data quickly), you may be able to research prior awards of the contract or of similar contracts, who won them, at what prices, and with what spare parts sales. If you have built adequate competitor files, you may have brochures, annual reports, competitors' proposals, and other such useful material in your own proposal library and swipe files, and they may be a source of the information you need.

You should have your own proposal library and computer database of proposal information. If you have built an adequate library and database, and have accumulated a good volume of in-house data, market research will get progressively less burdensome as your store of in-house data grows.

But you do have the right to know what the bottom line is, what the government is currently paying—with public money—for such items as those for which you contemplate bidding.

Still another cost item that can be useful to learn when bidding for an indefinite-quantity contract, especially one with many items of supply or services, is how much of each item the client has bought in previous years. Here is one example of how that information can become a strategy for success—a strategy for *appearing* to be a low bidder, even though you may not be.

In one contract for an annual ordering agreement, one of the many listed services was photography. However, when a prospective proposer looked over the list of rates and record of purchases made under previous contracts, he noticed that the agency had asked for and listed rates for photographic services, but had never bought any of these services. He inquired into this and learned that the agency had a large photo lab of its own, and handled all its own photography requirements. However, the agency carried the photo lab services item on its supply contract "just in case" it should be one day needed. He therefore decided that he could risk possible small losses by offering photo services very cheaply, since it was unlikely he would ever be asked to supply them. This enabled him to become the *apparent* low bidder, and he won the contract.

A similar set of conditions exists often in other indefinite-quantity, "laundry list" procurements, and this strategy has worked well in a number of cases. Technical services contracts sometimes call for quoting rates for the services of specialists of more than one level of experience and qualification. For example, an RFP may call for quoting hourly rates for Engineer I, Engineer II, Engineer III, and Engineer IV, with descriptions of the ranking and qualifications for each level. A proposer may decide, after reading these qualifications, that the project requires only three levels of engineers, and that he will not use the fourth (which may be any one of the levels). The proposer, planning to quote and manage every task with the other levels of engineers, then quotes a very low rate for the level he sees as unnecessary, and thus appears to be the low bidder.

In another kind of application, the client may call for the design and manufacture of some piece of equipment and require a list of spare parts and their prices. It is a fact of life that spare parts are necessary to maintain almost any item of equipment that is made up of many parts, and an institutional customer, such as a government agency or corporation, will normally stock a supply of spare parts. It is another fact of life that spare parts priced individually as replacements are always more expensive than those parts were when they were procured in bulk for the original manufacture of the equipment. The sales of spare parts are, in fact, generally much more profitable to the manufacturer than was the sale of the original equipment. Therefore, the order for spare parts to be purchased with or following the sale of the equipment is a great influence on the proposer's price. (It is analogous to the well-known story of King Gillette giving away razors to create a market for razor blades.) It is therefore not unusual for proposers to quote prices at or even slightly below breakeven, if they are assured of a large order for spare parts. Unfortunately, such procurements often do not specify any guaranteed number of spares to be bought. This creates a dilemma for the proposer, who now has no idea of what the gamble is in quoting at or below breakeven. The proposer then needs some reliable information on the probable spare parts sale. (Of course, the resourceful proposer may devise an alternative plan that includes provision for spare parts and an attractive price as an inducement.)

Asking Questions: An Exception

I have made much in earlier pages of being careful to ask the client no questions whose answers would be helpful to everyone who requested a copy of the RFP. That includes most questions pertaining to the work specified in the RFP because the client will take the position that everyone is entitled to the same information in the SOW. As with most "rules," there are a few exceptions.

In my experience, for example, when I requested access to public information under authority of the Freedom of Information Act, I got the information I asked for but there was no move to disseminate that to others because it was public information. I did not gain any special advantages over competitors by asking for information that was as easily available to them and to everyone else as it was to me.

I also found that much the same philosophy applied to asking about any policies of the contracting office. (Actually, they are usually policies of the contracting official, but it is much more discreet to make the query impersonal by phrasing it as office policies.) For example, in pondering the bid/no-bid decision of a certain services contract that was to be on a cost-plus basis, we were totally in the dark on pricing. Finally, we decided to simply call and ask whether the contracting office had a policy regarding fees on cost-plus work. The response was a prompt one in a cheery voice: "We sure do. It's 9 percent as the maximum."

Calling the program people directly and asking questions about the requirement after the RFP has been sent to you is taboo and can get you promptly disqualified from the competition. At this stage, all questions must be directed to the contracting officer, who will pass your question on to the program office for response. The response will come back to you and all others via the contracting office, if there is to be additional information provided. However, you can ask the contracting officer directly any questions he or she can answer directly, such as policy questions, how many copies of the RFP have been sent out, whether a list of RFP requesters will be made available, or others concerned with contracting matters and not program matters. You may or may not get answers to these questions, according to the policies and practices of the contracting office. Surprisingly often, however, this simple action of asking innocent but judicious questions produces excellent results with no downside to the action.

Using Help-Wanted Advertising as an Intelligence-Gathering Method

There are many kinds of information you need, of course, and many methods for gathering useful information. They range from obvious and simple methods to sophisticated and highly complex ones. For example, to bid for a Postal Service on-site contract that would require several technicians to be employed at the USPS main supply depot in Topeka, Kansas, the successful bidder ran help-wanted advertisements in a Topeka newspaper, with responses to be directed to a box number at the newspaper. Once responses had been accumulated, the bidder sent someone to Topeka to interview applicants, and collect information on relevant salary requirements there, and choose a tentative staff, with their résumés. That armed the proposer with specific costs and a set of résumés to offer in the proposal (which proved to be a winner, fortunately).

Many government installations are Government Owned, Contractor Operated (GOCO) facilities. A GOCO contract for a large NASA installation that employed several hundred people near Washington, D.C., came up for renewal. The RFP did not reveal a great deal of detail about the installation. One contractor, seeking information to determine whether to incur the expense of preparing a large and costly proposal, ran several help-wanted advertisements designed to attract people with such skills as would be appropriate to the kind of work done at that installation. The advertisements requested that résumés be submitted.

The advertisements drew many responses from employees of the incumbent contractor operating the site. From those letters and résumés alone, the advertiser gained a great deal of information about the operation and could infer much about the incumbent's contract. He fleshed that knowledge out with skillful interviews of a number of the respondents, and before long he had built such a detailed picture of the site and its operation that he knew almost as much about the operation as the manager of the site did. He knew or could estimate such facts as the number of people employed there, the size of the contract, and the client-contractor relationships that gave him insight into the client's probable desires regarding the outcome of the proposal competition. Subsequent developments proved that he was right in these judgments. (As a bonus, he also now had a stack of résumés of highly qualified employees to retain or hire if he competed for and won the contract.)

The Need to Read Carefully—and Then Read Again!

Careful study of the SOW is itself an intelligence-gathering measure, too often underused by proposal writers. One excellent example of such use of an RFP arose from a requirement for a GOCO contract to run a small government office cataloging parts at a NASA facility. It was a quite small contract, but the principle would be valid for contracts of much larger size.

The successful proposer for this small contract recognized that this was an ongoing on-site program, with an incumbent contractor.

Obviously, the contract had reached the end of its three-year term and was up for renewal, which required open bidding. The RFP did not stipulate the number of people employed at the cataloging office. It appeared obvious to him from this and other clues that the RFP was wired—slanted for the incumbent as a contractor favored by the agency to keep the contract. The client showed little inclination to furnish any more information than was absolutely necessary. Thus, instead of estimating total work hours or providing other indirect information on staffing, the statement used the roundabout method of specifying a representative quantity of cataloging information to be performed each year. Too, when this proposer asked to visit the site, he was stalled with one excuse after another to postpone and delay such a visit. The procurement certainly appeared to be wired for the incumbent contractor. This proposer was not discouraged, however. He knew that sometimes wired RFPs can be unwired, and he was not yet ready to pass on this one or to protest it. (A protest did not appear to offer much benefit here, except to probably extend the incumbent's contract for several months while the protest was adjudicated.) From the information provided, however, the proposer could estimate that the work represented about one and one-half man-years of cataloging work, and thus only two people were required to get the job done. Still, however, he did not know how many were actually stationed there by the incumbent contractor.

Stubborn and persistent study of the SOW finally produced the answer. Buried in multiple paragraphs of text were scattered mentions of three job titles: manager, secretary, and cataloger, revealing a staff of three. The revelation probably was unintentional, but it was just compensation for the proposal writer's efforts. The resulting proposal won the contract with an indisputable argument for a staff of only two, a manager-cataloger and a secretary-cataloger. Although the contracting official did not appear to be highly pleased with the result, he had little recourse but to award the contract to the hard-working proposer.

On another occasion, where the RFP called for a laundry list of publications services and price was obviously going to be a key factor, diligent study revealed, buried in RFP pages supporting and expanding on the SOW, the client's definition of a page of manuscript.

Surprisingly, the definition described a far smaller page than is generally considered to be a de facto standard. This information allowed the proposer to lower its per-page bid, thereby winning the contract.

In yet another case, an RFP for reverse engineering services, emanating from the night vision laboratory, a military unit at Fort Belvoir, Virginia, included a requirement that the contractor's site for carrying out the contract be located within a 45-mile radius of Fort Belvoir. The successful proposer was located in Rockville, Maryland, and when the inspection team arrived to verify the existence of a satisfactory facility to perform the work, they said that the proposer did not meet the 45-mile requirement, which they had measured as 65 miles in driving from Fort Belvoir to Rockville. The contractor had anticipated that and was ready for it, having done his homework. He responded that the only way to measure the distance was on the map with a ruler, inasmuch as the RFP used the word *radius*, which is a straight-line distance between two points! Mileage by road was thus irrelevant. He was awarded the contract without further discussion.

The Grapevine

There is a grapevine in every field. The larger and more far-flung the field, the larger and more far-flung is the grapevine. Frequently, when I was at a loss for useful information regarding a procurement contract I was considering pursuing, I got my most valuable intelligence from the grapevine, from friends and acquaintances who were in similar enterprises and gathering their own intelligence. So the grapevine is not always a rumor mill; it is often a casual way of sharing information through an informal network of people talking about a subject of common interest. Some of the gossip is accurate and reliable intelligence; some is not. You must use judgment—sound common sense—in evaluating any gossip you get on the grapevine to determine whether it is likely to be accurate intelligence or only mindless and unreliable rumor. You must try to confirm the information. A few measures you can use to guide your judgment in reviewing and assessing information you get are:

- Is the report compatible with other information you have gathered?
- Does it make good sense to you on the face of it or in terms of anything else you know?
- Can you get confirmation, such as similar reports from other independent sources?
- Is the source usually reliable? Someone you know? A complete stranger and unknown quantity?
- Is there great risk in trusting and acting on the report? (What are the worst possible consequences?)
- Is it possible that this is misinformation—deliberately misleading gossip? (Don't discount the possibility.)

To use any grapevine, you must be part of it, a functioning part. This means that you must be a source, too; you must give up something. (Is there not always a price to pay for anything you want?) Usually, as common sense dictates, this will be information that will not in any way compromise or threaten your own competitive position. That is, you may pass on information you have about procurements that you do not intend to pursue or information that in no way compromises your competitive position on procurements you do intend to pursue. For example, someone I know may be able to tell me who I will be facing as competition for a given project I intend to pursue. Someone on the grapevine may claim that a certain corporation (or individual) is a shoo-in for the job. Or I hear how difficult or how easy it is to deal with the client in question. Of course, this may also be misinformation, as noted above, designed to weaken your position as a contender for the contract, so you exercise some judgment in receiving and acting on the information.

On balance, intelligence that comes to you via the grapevine is most valuable when it can be confirmed or it confirms and is compatible with something else you know, or when you know and trust the source. It is least reliable when it stands alone, with no other corroborating information, and is from a source about which or whom you know little or nothing. At its best, it is most useful as reinforcement of other information, but there are occasions when it is your only source and represents all you can get about some aspect of a procurement. You must, in that case, decide whether acting on the information is a good gamble.

When Marketing Intelligence Changes the Rules

There is a possibility of intelligence-gathering operations that we have not considered at all. We have been discussing intelligence gathering in terms of how it may aid us in formulating strategies for winning. But is it possible that intelligence you gain may affect your entire approach to responding? May it change your views of the procurement vis-à-vis your reaction to the RFP?

Of course, it may do exactly that. It may cause you to "fall back and regroup"—to reconsider not only your possible approach to the proposal, but your approach to whether or not to write a proposal. If you learn that some contractor is considered almost certain to be awarded the contract, regardless of competitive proposals, and you find that assessment to be reliable, you may decide to no-bid the RFP.

In short, rather than using intelligence only as a method for making the best proposal, turn to the grapevine early to help make the decision whether to respond with a proposal. In fact, marketing intelligence is or ought to be an ongoing activity that begins in the preproposal phase (see Chapter 2) when the decision is being made to consider responding with a proposal.

Mailing Lists

Today, with the ready availability of e-mail and those spontaneous discussions carried on by e-mail exchange via what are known as "mailing lists," such informal networks are present in great numbers on the Internet.

The Web is a useful place for finding relevant mailing lists, and there are new lists starting almost continuously. In fact, you may want to launch one of your own. Search engines such as Alta Vista, Lycos,

Yahoo, and others will help you find Web sites and mailing lists of interest, sites and lists dealing with proposal writing per se, with government and private-sector contracting, with independent consulting and contracting, and with various other relevant subjects. Experts and information abound worldwide on and via the Internet. So far, I have rarely failed to get at least some of the information I was seeking by turning to these sources for direction or for a starting point.

The Proposal Library

Any organization that frequently writes proposals should have an organized and ever-growing proposal library or data bank as a major receptacle of and resource for marketing intelligence. Most of the information gathered about clients, competitors, projects, and other relevant subjects is worth keeping. I have written many book proposals, and not too long ago one of my publishers, a large corporation, turned to me for copies of two of my old contracts that had somehow departed their files, and which they needed to perform a service I had requested. Fortunately, I have kept a firm grip on such assets, and I was able to accommodate them and my own interests with copies of those two contracts. As discussed earlier, you should develop your own research sources. Some material that ought to be collected and stored in the proposal library are:

- A file of your own past proposals, successful and not successful
- Copies of competitors' proposals
- Intelligence reports gathered in the past
- Your organization's own literature—brochures, catalogs, journal articles, and other material
- Competitors' literature of the same nature
- Articles about your organization, competitor organizations, and your industry
- Books and periodicals relevant to proposal needs

The second item, copies of competitors' proposals, are usually the most difficult of all the above items to get. You can request copies of competitors' winning proposals under the Freedom of Information Act, but copies of the original, unexpurgated editions are much better to have. Competitors' proposals that did not win are more difficult to get, but are also most useful. Over time, a few of them will drift into your possession, sometimes from a former employee of a competitor who is now your employee, sometimes from the discarded trash of a client organization, sometimes via some mysterious transit, and sometimes via your own staff people who have worked in the past for competitors and kept samples of their past proposal work. Take advantage of all opportunities to add to this collection. A single copy in a single procurement may be the key to a major contract.

Presumably, intelligence reports of the past will be in computer form and can be stored in your computer system with a suitable search engine for convenience in finding specific information. In fact, for the greatest efficiency in storing as much searchable data as possible, such as journal articles and paper-only proposals, scan and store them as computer files.

Relevant trade shows and conferences offer a good opportunity to collect materials for your library and to gather useful information in general. Someone familiar with your proposal library and its needs should attend such functions and collect useful materials.

6

Page-Limited Proposals

Background of Page Limitations in Proposal Requests

Some RFPs impose a limitation on the number of pages you are allowed to present in your proposal. Do not ever set out to write a proposal that will fit the page limitation. Instead, write a proposal that will offer a complete program and present all the arguments necessary to sell the program, regardless of how many pages that requires. Then edit the proposal to fit within the stated limitation. A client's page limitation may cause immediate suspicion by some contractors that the proposal is "wired," stacking the deck to give a favored contractor an edge by prearranged understanding. In fact, the page limitation is usually an honest effort to keep all proposals within reasonable limits of size and coverage. The good news is that this problem can and should be made to turn out to be a boon rather than a curse. Handled well, a page limitation can result in a far better proposal than would otherwise have been the case. Answering these proposals often proves that excellent writing and editing skills are as important as marketing skills.

Some proposal writers apparently believe that the larger their proposals are, the more impressive they are. They therefore overwrite quite heavily, even deliberately. They often add lengthy and unnecessary documentation, and include page after page of footnotes, other citations, and thick appendixes. Even those writers who do not deliberately try to overwhelm a client with their arguments tend to overwrite, especially when writing to sell something.

Verbosity is symptomatic of many who are not especially skilled or experienced as writers, but the tendency is not exclusively their characteristic. Although even highly experienced professional writers overwrite in their drafts, they are aware that they do so and accept it as characteristic of a first draft. Unfortunately, because the majority of those who write proposals or portions of proposals are not experienced career writers, they also are not experienced in editing and refining the product to produce a terse, effective proposal.

Why Page Limitations?

In a given procurement, a client may receive a hundred or more proposals. Coping with such a tidal wave of words and data is an awesome challenge for clients. To discourage a tidal wave of words in proposal presentations, clients sometimes limit the number of pages a proposal may contain. At the same time, they specify maximum allowable page sizes and minimum, noncondensed font sizes to prevent writers from nullifying the limitation. Even further, they often cover what you may or may not include as appended material or exhibits, charts, audiotapes, videotapes, photographs, and computer disks. These may be limited, completely barred, or admissible only under certain specified limitations. Here we will assume that all these prohibitions have been expressed, so you must meet the page limitation by managing the volume of text.

Your problem as a proposer faced with a page limitation is to present a complete program and necessary sales arguments within the boundaries of the limitation. At first, you may view the page limitation as a hindrance to presenting your case in its entirety. The resourceful proposal team, however, reads the wording of the page limitation instructions very carefully, at least as carefully as you read the SOW. The instructions may exclude certain items such as personnel résumés from the limitation and permit you to be as detailed about résumés as you wish. Some may permit appended material without restriction. Once you know what you can and cannot include, you can manage not only your words, but where they appear. You can optimize your selling opportunities and stay within the limits.

The Most Basic Remedy: Effective Editing and Revision

Getting rid of all the excess verbiage that is common in first drafts of almost anything written is often the only measure necessary to meet the page limitation. It requires skills in writing, rewriting, and marketing to decide what is necessary and what is not. This is not to say that the overwriting most of us do in our first drafts is a bad thing. Allow yourself free rein to write your first draft in exhaustive detail and at great length, regardless of what the final intended length of the product is to be. A large portion of any credit given for good writing should be allocated to skillful editing based on prioritizing what is important to the client and rewriting to the strongest marketing features.

Editing enables you to evaluate what you have as you edit and rewrite—the facts, the arguments, the strengths, and the weaknesses—so that you may select and keep the best of it discriminatingly. You should, of course, expect to do at least two drafts, a rough one and a revised one, although the best written products are almost always the fruit of many drafts and revisions. Only neophyte and overly optimistic writers expect to get it all right in the first draft, much less actually produce their best writing in a first draft.

All of this is true for writing in general, but proposal writing is a special case. Their deadlines are often formidably short. Most proposal efforts are carried out under intense deadline pressure to design, document, and argue a custom program. A major objective of editing and revision generally is elimination of unnecessary material and trimming of fat—elimination of material of secondary importance, if and as necessary to stay within the page limits. The second objective is to ensure good organization, smooth and logical transitions, and check spelling, grammar, and punctuation. Every writer should do as much self-editing as possible, but having an experienced editor work over the entire draft after the writer's self-editing is a good idea. That is not only because some writers are not effective editors, but also because it is difficult for any writer to slash his or her own work.

What Can Be and Should Be Cut?

Two classes or categories of material that can be cut are

1. excessive and unnecessary verbiage in general, and
2. excessive and unnecessary sales presentations and arguments.

The two are different, and yet they are related. Let's talk first about reducing verbiage, a basic editorial skill.

Editing, even self-editing, is usually done in at least two stages, because it is difficult to edit a manuscript for all things at the same time. The first reading/editing should correct obvious faults of language usage—grammar, spelling, punctuation—and slash unnecessary words and phrases. For example, "in order to" can almost always be shortened to "to" without losing any meaning or effect. It also makes for brisker style, of course, even though that is not the immediate purpose. The second stage is to weigh the content to see what passages can be eliminated, if any, with no significant loss of important information and details. Here are a few ideas that will help:

- A page-limited proposal is not the place to show off an extensive vocabulary. Use the simplest language possible. Use not only the simplest sentence structures, but the most common words (words that do not need explanation). This has nothing to do with words being short or long in the sense of letters and syllables, but only in being easily understood by the intended reader. A word that is short but uncommon, such as "oblate," is a "big word" and almost compels you to add something parenthetically to ensure that the reader understands.
- Be wary of the appearance of all footnotes, parenthetical excursions, and other references. Do not retain them without some

powerful reasons for doing so. They may make your proposal appear scholarly, but they can almost always be shortened or dispensed with entirely.

- Be alert for possible redundancies. Even when a single writer develops an entire proposal, many redundancies creep in, and the appearance of redundancies is even more probable when a number of writers contribute to a proposal. Screen carefully for material that appears more than once without a compelling reason for its repeated appearance. (See section later on cross-referencing.)
- The use of telegraphic style, one in which nouns and adjectives are used sparingly, and verbs all but eliminated, is often possible and appropriate. It can be highly effective in economizing on sentence lengths and page counts. Use it wherever possible.
- Make bulleted lists, such as this. Like telegraphic style (which is itself appropriate use for such lists), it offers opportunities to economize on words.
- Keep staff résumés to one page, maximum, and shorter if possible. Frequently, it is possible to use a style for résumés that permits presenting two on a page. Present only the facts most pertinent to the project—and include the résumés of only key staff (senior people) proposed for the project.

A word of caution: Use the checklists and flowchart you created for the project to be sure that you have not eliminated anything the RFP requires. You must manage to meet the page limitation without compromising complete responsiveness to the RFP. Items that represent response to the mandates of the RFP are "untouchables" in the editing process. Be careful to ensure that when you edit them for conciseness they are still fully responsive to the mandates of the RFP.

Another consideration is to determine what text is least important from the marketing viewpoint. What details of the marketing presentations and arguments, for example, would represent the lowest gain? Make value judgments on the marketing importance of various presentations. Continue paring only as long as necessary to meet the mandated limit.

Using Illustrations, Tables, and Matrices

A proposal is a communication, and that does not restrict you to words alone. Words, are, in fact, one of the poorer means of communication. Illustrations and tables are more effective and more efficient means to convey some kinds of information. They require far less paper for presentation. And visual communication is often far more effective in driving home important points and making complex concepts understandable to the reader almost instantaneously.

A good illustration is one that tells a story in less space than its written explanation would take. It does so by being self-explanatory. A worthy illustration requires little or no accompanying textual explanation and should require only a brief introduction.

There are many ways to make an illustration self-explanatory. The first and most direct way is to present it at the right place in the text, with the right introduction. For greatest economy of words and space, rather than introducing an illustration with something such as "See Figure X for an explanation," use a simple parenthetical mention, such as (Figure X). The figure itself will have the title or legend "Example of Classroom Organization." That is a more efficient use of the figure, and saves words in making the reference.

Label functions and other items in the figure, where appropriate, to minimize the need for textual explanations. Study your text, and if you find that you are devoting passages of text to explain your illustrations, take measures to reduce or eliminate that text. See, for one, if any of the text is redundant with information already available in the illustration itself. If the text cannot be eliminated or reduced, study the illustration carefully to see if you can get the key information into the figure itself by using labels and call outs, or even by making revisions to the illustration. The capability of the illustration to explain itself is a direct measure of its quality: The more appropriate the illustration, the less the textual explanation required, other than titles or legends. An illustration that requires a great deal of text is not necessarily a badly executed illustration; it may be simply a badly chosen one. Overall, do not accept the needless redundancy of illustrations that must be carefully explained in the text. Keep the need to reduce text in mind as you select your illustrations.

Make illustrations only as large as they need to be. With modern computer composition, it is usually possible to manage the size of the illustration quite easily. Frequently, illustrations contain unnecessary detail, and can be cropped and sized accordingly.

The flowchart you developed earlier to reflect what you propose to deliver is an illustration. It can present the heart of your proposal, the proposed program, in a few pages, minimizing the amount of text required, and maximizing space to devote to sales arguments and success strategies. In addition, other flowcharts and/or organization charts may help minimize textual descriptions and explanations. Consider the use of simple charts to replace pages of text.

All the same considerations apply to the use of tables and matrices, which also greatly reduce the amount of verbiage required. In some cases, such a table or matrix is more effective and more appropriate than an illustration would be. Tables and matrices are not necessarily presentations of numbers. Many kinds of textual material can also be reduced to more efficient tabular presentations. If there is repetitiveness of text expressions and/or there are textual comparisons and correlations to be made, there is an excellent possibility that a space-saving table or matrix can be developed to deliver the information far more efficiently and with a far more useful presentation. Figure 6.1 illustrates the principle. It is a hypothetical accounting of the kinds of contracts you have had with government agencies. This is a simplified example. The actual case would probably be a much larger chart that listed contract numbers and names of government project managers (or contracting officers' technical representatives) and other details documenting the proposer's experience. Of course, this presentation also may be done as a spreadsheet.

Cross-Referencing

It is easy to slip into redundancy in any expository writing where some subject must be referred to at more than one point. Here, cross-referencing may be employed to save space, even if it is less convenient for the reader than repeating the original information. In

Figure
6.1

Sample Space-Saving Table or Matrix

Contracting Experience with Federal Agencies

Agency	Training	Publications	Audio/Visuals
IRS	X	X	—
OPM	X	—	X
DOL	—	X	—
USDA	X	—	X
FCC	—	X	—
BuPers	X	X	—
GSA/PBS	X	X	X

reviewing and editing an earlier draft, be alert for redundancies and consider cross-referencing as a way to minimize space required. Instead of repeating the information, refer the reader to it with a brief parenthetical reference such as this: (Page 72) or (Section III).

Last Resort

What the government refers to as a "competitive proposal" is a "negotiated procurement." That is, unlike the sealed-bid procurement, where the lowest bid wins the contract, a competitive proposal chosen as the best one is not automatically a winner. It is a leading candidate for contract negotiation, which must be conducted successfully before a contract can be awarded. (For small contracts, "negotiation" may be only a brief telephone conversation to affirm the terms, but it still qualifies as a negotiation.) On the other hand, the client often avoids the use of the word *negotiation* (probably as a psychological negotiating tactic to avoid having the contractor become overly optimistic and thus a tougher negotiator) and simply asks the proposer to come to a meeting, where the proposer will be asked to discuss his or her proposal, answer questions about it, invited to submit a best and final offer, and permitted (or invited) to file a supplement to the original proposal. Even that latter element of "permitting" or "inviting" you to submit a supplement, rather than requiring it, is a good negotiating tactic for the client, because it avoids giving you any solid idea of the client's intentions or your position vis-à-vis winning the award. Ordinarily, such meetings are conducted by the contracting official, although the program office is represented at the table also, and this itself is an indication that negotiation is the purpose of the meeting.

What this means is that it is possible to finesse the page limitation in another way, using this alternative avenue to negotiation to do so. When and if you encounter a dead end—where you have material you believe to be highly favorable to the effectiveness of your presentation but you cannot fit it in under the limitation—there is a possible alternative. Present the material in a clearly labeled brief summary that states you will be pleased to present a more complete coverage of the subject by any means the client chooses, such as a written addendum to the proposal or an oral presentation. (This is making lemonade out of the lemon!)

This approach has a side benefit of encouraging a special response from the client, often an invitation to negotiate or a request to meet as a preliminary to negotiations, regarding subjects that will be discussed in detail later, in contexts that have nothing to do with page limitations. (Some of the related subjects present highly useful strategies in general for responses to certain kinds of requirements.) Bear in mind that the entire process is, as stated, a negotiated procurement. Therefore, even though the RFP may mandate a page limitation, the client is free to ask questions and solicit additional material from you as an amendment or supplement to your proposal, in the course of follow-up discussions of any kind.

In one case, for example, the client, a military agency, wanted to contract for a training manual on security. A proposer who thought it would be helpful to his sales arguments to cite certain passages from security regulations found it impossible to do so under the page limitations mandated by the RFP. He therefore summarized each such regulation in a single sentence or two, but provided complete identification of each regulation's page and paragraph numbers, knowing the client could look them up easily.

In another case, the proposer was to write and submit a book in camera-ready form to the Government Printing Office. The proposer found the RFP lacked most of the detailed specifications necessary to either establish the scope of effort or price the job. She therefore explained the dilemma briefly and suggested a minimal set of specifications, but pointed out other possible approaches that she would be happy to furnish as alternatives.

7

Presentation Strategies: I

How Important Is the Presentation Strategy?

The strategy of a presentation has more than one aspect. There is the visual impact, for one, the impact of a first impression. The government enjoins all who respond to their RFPs to avoid unnecessarily elaborate and costly presentations and warns that such a presentation will be interpreted as a lack of cost consciousness. Still, few proposers take that too seriously. What is excessively elaborate and costly? There are no standards or guidelines, and so it becomes an entirely subjective matter, and most proposers do try to submit proposals that are colorful and highly professional in appearance so as to make them distinctive and impressive in overall appearance. Besides, the proposer is making a decision on how to spend its own money—not the client's.

While presenting a good looking proposal will not get you a contract, there is a great benefit to be gained from making a memorable first impression. A first objective in making any advertising or sales presentation is to get attention. (You cannot deliver a message without getting attention, and you are almost always competing with others and their presentations for attention.) In at least one case in my experience, I was able to verify the downside of not making a memorable impression.

Long after losing a bid proposal, I had the opportunity to do some consulting work for the chief evaluator of the proposals in that competition. I persuaded him to make an unofficial review of the old proposal, which, fortunately, he still had in his office. He assured me that it was as good a proposal as the one he had chosen for award, but it had probably been "lost" in the crush of reading a large number of submitted proposals. Because of circumstances at the time, I had been forced to prepare my proposal by the simplest means possible: a portable typewriter, ordinary office stationery, a copying machine, and a common stapler—not the ideal tools for making a proposal even slightly memorable in appearance.

A proposal that is highly distinctive and memorable also offers the important advantage of having a distinct aura of professional polish. This includes not ink, paper, and bindings alone, but the quality of the writing—in organization, smooth transitions, lucid expositions, well conceived illustrations, logical flow, and the marketing points to choose your proposal. Combine these traits with a pleasing and noteworthy physical appearance, and how could any reader not take note and be well enough impressed to remember this proposal?

Writing Strategies

The act of writing involves strategies—techniques for producing the best copy in the most efficient way. Bear in mind always that a proposal is written under a deadline that is inviolable and unforgiving. (Extensions sometimes occur, but do not count on the possibility.) Missing the deadline—even by minutes—makes the proposal worthless and wastes the effort and clever thinking that went into developing whatever it presented. You must learn how to write well when there is not enough time—not enough time to do it over, so you must somehow make the time available to do it "right." As we discuss the strategies of presentation, we shall include some appropriate writing strategies.

Some organizations that write proposals daily, and often have more than one proposal in process at any given time, have formats carefully designed to create maximum impact. These formats are similar to those used in the commercial book publishing world, with such refinements as drop capitals, stylized type (especially headline type), blurbs, glosses, and other typographical and presentation refinements. These are a great help to writers, especially those with little writing experience, in helping them focus their work and improve the quality of their writing. Later, you will find a suggested proposal format that is generalized enough to lend itself easily to any special format. In any case, the explanations accompanying the outline will help you find the immediate objectives for each section and subsection.

Attention-Getting Covers

As a general strategy, you should try to make every proposal an attention-getting, memorable presentation. A distinctive cover may contribute effectively to that end. A metallic gold cover distinguished one proposal that I recall, and drew a great deal of attention and comment. A relevant illustration on the cover will draw some notice. In at least one case, we used a foldout cover. In the case referred to, the illustration was a flow diagram in pictorial style, the function of each box presented by an icon—a computer, a letter, a magnifying glass, or other device, labeled if necessary. The cover unfolded to reveal the entire drawing.

One proposer made a practice of printing the client's logo boldly on the cover. And some proposers find and print, on the cover and as a running head or foot in the proposal, an acronym or brief phrase that dramatizes their overall proposal strategy or some important and prominent feature of their proposed program. They stand out by focusing on the client rather than the proposer's logos, trade names, or slogans.

Thus it is often difficult to separate presentation strategy from program strategy, and you will find discussions in this chapter relating to both. However, although it is normally the first thing the customer sees when picking up your proposal to read it, the cover is only one element of your proposal. Each element and area of your proposal is itself a candidate to play a role in your strategy overall by being based on a strategy of its own.

The Strategy of the Introduction

If you were a sales representative calling on a prospect for the first time, you would normally introduce yourself and the company you represent, explain your product or service briefly, and then make a serious effort to learn the prospect's problems, worry items, and perceived needs. You would then try to win an order by suggesting how your product or services would solve those problems and satisfy those needs. That is an act of consulting, and good salespeople find that consulting of this kind is an excellent way to win sales. The salesperson may or may not always be greeted warmly, but the friendly problem solver and good listener is always welcome.

Your technical proposal is your sales representative. It also must

- introduce you—your organization and product or service in general;
- offer a brief introduction to your general interest and qualifications;
- identify the RFP and the requirement—the client's need to which you are responding;
- discuss the need and the best approach to satisfying it;
- present your proposed program—the details of how you will satisfy the client's want; and
- provide your credentials and qualifications to do the job.

You can be—ought to be—a consultant and problem solver via your proposal.

For small tasks, this written proposal may be in the form of a letter of a few pages. For larger projects, the proposal may require several dozen pages as a bound volume. And for really large projects, the proposal may run to two or more volumes. For purposes of discussion, we will talk in terms of a small to medium-size project requiring a technical proposal of several dozen pages. We will assume, too, that the technical proposal and cost proposal are separate documents, as they are required to be in government procurements (although this may not be the case in procurements by private-sector companies and corporations).

Important Differences Between Government and Private-Sector Bids

The differences between marketing to government agencies and marketing to private-sector business organizations are relatively superficial, especially as more and more government procurement is of standard commercial products, purchased under commercial policies and practices, using standard commercial terms. There is one highly important difference that will not change: Private-sector organizations may buy what they want, from whomever they want, when they want, and at whatever prices they want. Government agencies must follow procurement procedures dictated by the Federal Acquisition Regulations (FAR), and spend only what has been authorized by law for whatever products and services have been authorized by law. To be maximally effective in proposal writing, you should have a good grasp of the laws and regulations governing procurement practices and procedures. That knowledge can be a major element in developing winning arguments and strategies.

Another important difference is that when you propose to private-sector organizations and executives who know you from previous business associations, you need not describe your qualifications and credentials in detail to prove your capability to do the work required. In the commercial world, even if prospective clients do not know you or anything about you, they always tend to assume that if you are in a given field, you must be competent in that field. So they normally do not require any special evidence of your credentials. (Of course, the fact that a client does not demand to know your credentials does not mean that you should not offer them.) Government agencies, however, must evaluate your proposal objectively, per prescribed criteria, and can credit you only with what is stated in your proposal and can be verified, and not from what they happen to know or have heard about you, even from recent or current contracts with you. In proposing competitively to government agencies, therefore, you must always include a full account of your credentials, as prescribed in the RFP, no matter how well known you are to the agency. The failure to do this has cost more than one company a contract they otherwise had all wrapped up.

Proposal Formats

The client may mandate a specific proposal format, and in this computer age may even ask for or invite the proposal or elements of it to be in some computer medium, such as a floppy disk or CD ROM. In most cases, the RFP prescribes the information to be supplied and leaves the format of the proposal to the respondent. However, those organizations who award contracts regularly sometimes have their own chosen proposal format and insist that you follow it. Too, proposal requests call for custom work and often for creative work to produce unique designs. The characteristics or other considerations of a given procurement may therefore influence the format of the proposal and make it difficult to use a standard format. A proposal format must be flexible and easily adapted to the needs of any given requirement.

Some proposers try to follow the sequence of presentation used in the RFP in designing the format of their proposals. This rarely works out well. Often the RFP is not that well organized, and even when it is, the organization may not be the most effective for your purposes in writing a proposal. The objective of a proposal design should never be to choose the easy way, but to choose the way most likely to sell the client and win the contract.

Following is an outline of the technical proposal format suggested for general use and to be employed for reference here. Front matter will vary, according to the user's preferences, and there may or may not be back matter. Front and back matter elements will be discussed later. The format is a logical sequence for the presentation of the various elements normally required in a proposal, but the discussions will not be written in that same sequence, nor even discussed in that sequence. It would not make sense to attempt to write the Executive Summary before writing what is to be summarized, for example, and the same reasoning applies to discussions here.

The titles or headings for the sections or subsections are arbitrary, of course. Those used here are generic ones for descriptive purposes only and are not intended to be used as the headings in your own proposals. In fact, I would suggest that you do not use these because they are generic, and you can do better in most cases, producing hard-hitting headings that say something. In fact, I would make it a rule to shun boilerplate headings and titles and, instead, customize them for each given proposal. It is a good idea to make maximum use of every element of the proposal, including choosing titles, headings, and subheadings that help you sell the proposed program, as well as describe what you offer. Banish such generic, say-nothing headings as "General" and "Introduction" from your proposal vocabulary. They are throwaway headings—neglected opportunities to add weight to your proposal by sending messages with your headings, titles, and legends. "About the Offeror," for example, might better be "About [your company name]." Or, even better, something along the lines of "What [your company name] Has to Offer [client's name]." Still more powerful might be "What [your company name] Promises to Do for [client's name]." Or, if you have some special attention-getter to offer, this may be a good place to introduce it. If you have some well-known expert ready to consult with you on the project, you might mention that in a heading, such as "Project to be Supported by [name]." Anything extraspecial that you will offer may be advertised here. In one case, the proposer had it on good authority that the client was unhappy with the incumbent contractor and would be favorable to a change. The proposer headed his first section, "A New Broom." Not only was this highly relevant, but would be appropriate even if the information was wrong and the client was not unhappy with the incumbent contractor: Who could object to the suggestion of sweeping clean? The title could thus be made to fit somewhere in almost any proposal.

Introducing sales arguments and inducements into your normal headings is one way to earn special attention for the arguments. In fact, you may want to create a heading designed especially to introduce and earn extra attention for the special features you offer. When you have something special to offer, you must make it clear to the reader that it is something special. (See also the discussion of the hook, following the outline, for more thoughts on this subject.)

Following is the suggested proposal format, with brief discussions where discussions are appropriate at this point.

Front Matter

- **Copy of letter of transmittal**
- **Foreword or Preface**
- **Executive Summary**
- **Table of Contents**
- **Conformance or Response Matrix**

I: Introduction

- **About the Offeror**: Brief introduction to your firm; thumbnail sketch of your company and its general qualifications, vis-à-vis the procurement; preliminary explanations of what your proposal will present in pages to come; and other opening statements, including a "hook" or USP.
- **Understanding of the Requirement**: Brief statement expressing your understanding of the requirement in your own language (do not echo the words of the RFP), leaving out extraneous discussion and focusing on the *essence* of the requirement, providing a bridge (transition) to the discussion to follow as Section or Chapter II. Another excellent place to present the hook.

II: Discussion

- **Technical Discussion**: Discussion of the requirement, expanding on the understanding subsection of the first section; analyzing and identifying problems; and exploring and reviewing possible approaches (with pros and cons of each). Include similar discussions of all relevant matters including technical, management, schedule, other important points, and worry items. Use discussion to logically approach the rationale of the approach you will offer.
- **Approach**: Culminate in a clear explanation of the approach selected, bridging directly into the next chapter, where the spe-

cific program will be described. Include or refer to any graphics found elsewhere in the proposal, especially the functional flowchart. Explain the approach and technical or program design strategy employed. Sell the proposed program. Make the emotional appeals (promises). Explain the superiority of the proposed program. Demonstrate the proposer's grasp of the problem, of how to solve it, and of how to organize the resources.

III: Proposed Project

- **Specifics**: Discuss staffing and organization (with organization chart). Submit résumés of key people, either here or later in this chapter, but at least introduced here by name and title.
- **Proposed Project Management**: List procedures, philosophy, methods, controls; relationship of project to parent organization, staff reporting order; proposed liaison with client; contract management; other information on technical and general/administrative management of project.
- **Labor Loading**: List and explain major tasks and estimated hours for each principal in each task (use tabular presentation), with totals of hours for each task and totals of hours for each principal staff member. Include chart to illustrate graphically.
- **Deliverable Items**: Specify, describe, quantify what is to be delivered.
- **Schedules**: Specify, using client need as basis. (Use milestone chart, if possible. See Figure 7.1.)
- **Résumés**: Résumés of key staff including their names and titles, and their assignments for this project.

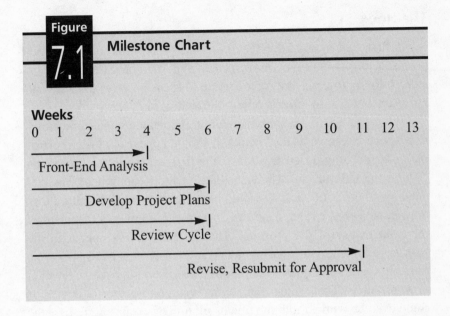

Figure 7.1   Milestone Chart

Weeks

0   1   2   3   4   5   6   7   8   9   10   11   12   13

Front-End Analysis

Develop Project Plans

Review Cycle

Revise, Resubmit for Approval

IV: Proposer's Qualifications

- **Description of Company**: Give a brief history. Describe facilities, relevant experience and achievements, past projects (especially those similar to one under discussion) history, and organization. Include corporate organization charts.
- **Facilities and Resources**: Physical facilities, key staff, résumés of non-key staff, testimonial letters, special awards, other pertinent facts.

Back Matter

- **Appendixes (citations, bibliography, other)**
- **Exhibits (drawings, photographs, tapes)**
- **Additional résumés (corporate people and/or possible backups)**

The Hook

A first goal in any advertising or sales promotion, including proposals, is to get attention. This can be an important factor in being considered for a project. Here we are going to focus on ways to command attention and arouse interest purely through writing skills.

What you use to get special attention immediately via some narrative device is known as the "hook." It should appear as close as possible to the opening. Logically, this is the first section in the subsection "About the Offeror" or "Understanding of the Requirement," as dictated by where it fits best. It would be better if it could be introduced or promised even earlier, as in the Executive Summary, an element of the front matter of the proposal. That is, there might appear in the Executive Summary an alerting notice as a teaser item of what is to be found in the first section of the proposal proper, with some suggestion of what this is. That would make it an even more powerful device. It could even be worked into the title or subtitle of the proposal, in some cases, and appear on the cover.

Another method that is not used often enough is to develop a logo that can be used as a part of the impact strategy and be reinforced on every page as a header or footer. This is an excellent way to employ a USP, for example, but any kind of message may be carried by this device. There are opportunities for at least four such messages: headers and footers on even-numbered pages and another pair on odd-numbered pages. Common usage of headers and footers is to identify the chapter or section on one page and the nearest heading on the facing page, but there is nothing sacred about this usage. Feel free to change that to whatever strikes you as a more helpful or persuasive strategy. If, for example, you offer some special feature you think must be impressed on the client's consciousness, you might use that as a header or footer. If you were trying to sell a fleet of cars, you might use "54 miles per gallon" as a header/footer.

There are several more elaborate devices or kinds of devices you might use here to gain attention and arouse interest early in the proposal. One is a brief introduction to or a hint of your main strategy. This can sometimes be worked in as part of the general coverage of what your proposal will present, as part of the first subsection, About the Offeror. Here are a few ideas of what this might be:

- The promise of some well-recognized, outstanding authority as a member of your proposed project staff or as a consultant to your project staff
- The promise of any other kind of unusual or exceptionally valuable resource to be used in the proposed project
- Some proprietary, special technique or methodology of your own invention
- An exceptional guarantee, pledge, or prediction
- A significant endorsement
- Some exceptionally significant or directly relevant experience of which you can boast
- A startling or extravagant promise you can support

It could be especially helpful to work something of the hook into the title of the section or subsection, as discussed earlier. On the other hand, some hook connected with your understanding of the requirement may be even more compelling and serve as excellent competitive strategy when it reflects an analysis and understanding that no one else has displayed. This subsection is a good place to introduce true independence of thought and innovation in your analysis of the client's need and the true problem. Remember that RFPs often describe only symptoms, and it falls to you to determine what the problem is or, if necessary, to demonstrate that the problem has yet to be defined and lay the groundwork for a discussion of how best to cope with the situation. Remember what your strategy is here: You wish to demonstrate to the client that you have a true understanding of the client's need or problem—not of the words in the RFP, and not of the symptoms described, but of the problem or need that can be logically inferred from those symptoms. Be cautious here! It is easy to get so eager to express your own ideas that they may come across as an attack on the writers and statements of the RFP, and so be offensive to the client. Use tact in critiquing or interpreting the RFP. Give a great deal of thought to how you express this.

In a great many cases, demonstrating your complete understanding of the requirement will compel you to go beyond what has been stated in the RFP. Often what the RFP describes are symptoms only, and you may have to do some preliminary analysis of those symptoms to arrive at a tentative definition of the problem. You may be able to bring about an "Aha!"—a sudden illumination for the client in that manner, and that would be an effective hook in itself. But be careful; it is easy to stub your toe here. If the client wants a training manual for students who may be fluent in Spanish or some other foreign language but illiterate in English (as was the case in an EPA requirement to train apartment house maintenance people), the temptation is to point out the foolishness of the idea. The smart approach, however, is to suppress that impulse. Ignore the anomaly completely, and offer a nonverbal system without comment on the fallacy of the client's original idea. (In the case referred to, so many unthinking proposers did embarrass the client with critical comments that the client felt compelled to cancel the procurement, planning to reissue it later as a requirement for a nonverbal training program.)

Note that we are still discussing here the first section of your proposal, which is to be introductory. You thus have a problem. You cannot do a truly effective job of meeting any of the objectives set forth for the introductory section until you have done a thorough analysis of the client's need and designed the program. You need to know just what you are introducing and defining. Therefore, the introduction is necessarily the last part written. It can be written effectively only after you have a complete description of what is to be introduced. A common practice is to draft an introduction and then revise it suitably later, after the body of the material has been written.

Aside from the fact that I need a lead when writing, as many writers do (in fact, it is known as "writing from the lead"), there is at least one great advantage to be gained in writing a rough draft of a first section. Writing that first section alerts you to the things you need to do later and conditions your mind to be watchful for and recognize those key items—perhaps even to develop them—as you proceed with the main body of the proposal. (At least, it has always worked that way for me.) In that respect, proposal writing is somewhat like chess to me: You must be thinking ahead and preparing for the end game.

There is also the inevitable downside, a hazard in rough-drafting an introduction at the beginning. Later, when you are engaged in the all-too-familiar eleventh-hour struggle to finish the proposal on schedule, you may very well completely forget that your introduction is only a rough draft, and let the proposal go out so handicapped. You can solve this problem by putting the draft in a typeface so different from the rest of the proposal that one glance tells you it is a draft. Or you may even find that under those eleventh-hour pressures, there is an irresistible temptation to save time by using the draft instead of writing a final version. It would be a mistake to do that, in all probability, for the introduction you would now write would be far different from this early draft. Beware of permitting this to happen.

I do have a remedy to offer for this problem. In practice, the needs of my first chapter are so much with me that I find or make time to return often to the draft of my first chapter and update it continually, as we refine the program and settle details. Thus, my draft first chapter is never very much out of step with the developing details of the main body of the proposal, but is continually growing closer and closer to whatever the final version ought to be. Perhaps I spend a little more time writing the introductory chapter by doing it that way, but it works well for me, often provoking new ideas, as I work, so I think that on the whole, it is an excellent way to develop the introduction. I suggest trying it.

The Client's General Concerns

Most clients have four general concerns, which may or may not be conscious points of address in their reading of your proposal, but will be items about which they will gain distinct impressions, as they make comparisons among the proposals submitted. If you are dealing with a government agency in a formal procurement, the evaluation criteria for your technical proposal will have been written with these points in mind:

- Your understanding of the requirement
- The quality of your proposed program
- The cost of your proposed program
- Your capability for implementing the proposed program
- The quality of the staff you propose
- Your dependability as a contractor
- Your ability to satisfy a special need

"Quality" may refer to a wide variety of factors, but usually refers to what appears to the client as some or all of the following in meeting the requirement:

- The perceived practicality and thus the probability of complete success of your program in satisfying the client's need
- Sophistication of design, or how your design compares with the client's own notions about the general approach to meeting the requirement
- What the client reads into the design as a reflection of your technical knowledge and capabilities
- The client's visceral reaction to an innovative design versus a tried and true or "old fashioned" approach to solving the problem

It is entirely possible, too, that the client will have retained a consultant expert to help him evaluate your proposal and make his or her own recommendations. (This is not an uncommon practice, and is often used in both government and commercial procurements.)

There is also prestige value to be considered as a possible concern of the client. The client may very well be concerned with the impression others get of the client's own taste and sophistication, as judged from the product. Therefore, one client may be glad to embrace a new and imaginative design as much as another client may shrink from attention-drawing boldness. Some clients want to be out front, bold, daring innovators, while others are fearful of failure and will always strongly prefer the conservative, "safe" approach.

It is always helpful to be conscious of possible mindsets of the client, so that you consider how your proposal language and possible connotations will affect the client. A single word can make a difference, as in the case of a project for a standard teleprinter in which a proposer's repeated stress on the word *monolithic* to summarize a major feature of the proposed design had a profound effect.

Cost is an obvious concern. If your cost estimate is priced beyond the client's budget's negotiable range, your proposal is doomed. On the other hand, if your price is too low, it will cast doubt on your understanding of the requirement, your capability, or the quality of what you will produce. The client may very well discard your proposal as unrealistic and unresponsive. In the case of government proposals, costs must be presented separately in a cost proposal, so the client may not yet be giving much thought to costs when studying your technical proposal, but at some point cost inevitably becomes a major concern, of course. However, even in reading your technical proposal, the question of cost may occur to the client if your proposed program appears to be overly elaborate or goes to the opposite extreme and appears to be too skimpy to do the job well. Despite the fact that costs must be presented in a separate document so that the technical proposal may be judged on its own merits without evaluators being influenced by costs, the reader of your proposal cannot help but get some idea of costs implied by your program description, especially in those areas where you quantify elements of your program, as you must if you are to prevent future disputes and protect yourself. (More on this later.)

The question of your capability for carrying out your proposed program is a common concern. Unfortunately, some proposals read very well, and offer what appears to be a sound or even superior program that ought to do the job very well, but the contractor proves to be someone who presents few qualifications to do the job. The writer of an excellent proposal may appear to be weak in experience or technical skills, lacking in qualified personnel to get the job done, with inadequate management and administrative plans, or otherwise deficient in resources. (Or the proposer may have hired experts to write the proposal.) Too, some contractors have little to offer but a small office and telephone—that is, they have few resources of their own for doing the work proposed. For example, there are contractors who plan to be middlemen or brokers. Their mode of operation is to win a contract and then subcontract virtually all of it to others who have the capabilities to do the work or they may even plan to sell (assign) the prime contract to someone. Experienced clients and their contracting experts soon get to know the "fingerprints" or distinctive style characteristics of most professional proposal writers and are not often deceived. Most clients will not knowingly welcome this kind of prime contractor.

It's not unknown for some contractors to be "good talkers," but poor "doers." That is, they can write a fine proposal, but they do not perform well. A client who has had experience with or knows of such contractors will be concerned with seeing some evidence of your dependability in carrying out the programs for which you contract: That client wants to see your track record. It is therefore common enough for an RFP to require an accounting of your past projects with names and telephone numbers of clients who can verify your claims in regard to having completed the projects successfully on schedule and within budget.

Where the program is labor intensive and requires staff with special capabilities, the perceived quality of the staff principals offered may be decisive. The client will evaluate your staff by reviewing their résumés, and so it would probably be a mistake to use boilerplate résumés here. The strategic thing to do is to customize the résumés of the proposed project principals to accentuate their skills and achievements most appropriate to the duties proposed for them for this project. It is probably a mistake to present résumés of several pages each, with all the tedious detail of irrelevant or only remotely relevant facts. In most cases, a single page will do, if the résumé is honed properly. In many cases, qualifications can be presented effectively in less than a full page.

A problem some clients encounter when contracting with large organizations is that their proposal promises the services of senior, highly qualified staff, but when they have been awarded the contract, they employ junior people to do the job. Some clients, aware that this is a possible problem, will stipulate in their RFP that the proposer must guarantee the services of the proposed staff or, if substitution becomes necessary, will provide substitutes of equal caliber. Some clients will go beyond this to stipulate further that the client reserves the right to see the résumés of all proposed substitutes and approve or reject them.

That consideration offers a possible strategy for the smaller organization, whether the client has made any relevant stipulations or not. The possibility of contracting with an organization who stipulates may be made into a worry item. The smaller organization may then make much of their size and point out that the client is assured of getting the services of the organization's principals, who are all of outstanding qualifications.

Occasionally, an RFP will have some extra-special requirement or difficult-to-satisfy need, and meeting it may be decisive. In some cases, the client is in straits and must have the project completed in record time, as was the case with a prime contractor who needed a training program to be written and presented "yesterday." (Accepting the impossible deadline for the project and explaining why the organization had a unique ability to meet this deadline was a very effective USP for this proposer.) Your proposal will therefore be evaluated in terms of your apparent ability to do the job quickly without sacrificing quality. In the case of one EPA procurement, the contractor was required to be able to supply highly qualified specialists quickly when called for by the client. The successful contender for the project satisfied this need by making arrangements with several universities and suppliers of professional temporaries, presenting letters from these sources verifying their support of the project. The ability to overcome difficulties, and the convincing presentation of evidence that you can do so, is the stuff of which proposal victories are made.

Proposal/Program Quality Begins with Problem Definition

Quality is always a difficult term to define because it is at best largely subjective. A client may have a few ideas of what would represent quality to him or her, but not be able to convey those ideas to proposers. In dealings with clients and prospective clients, there are always the critical matters of perception and credibility, and the client's idea of quality is very much related to these factors. Confront these issues early in the proposal, in the format outline presented here.

Many proposals are rejected as "nonresponsive," that is, as not addressing the client's problem as presented in the RFP. Often enough, as many as two-thirds of proposals submitted for a given project are rejected early in the evaluation process because the proposals showed little understanding of what the client wanted and needed. That may or may not be due to a proposer's actual lack of understanding of the requirement. It can be and sometimes is due to an exaggerated eagerness to sell one's pet solutions and so tend to see every client's need in that reference. But it may also be due to careless writing. Such writing does not specifically address the need to demonstrate a complete understanding, but starts with the assumption that the client has stated the problem clearly enough in the RFP and nothing more need be said about that. These are proposers who launch abruptly into the proposal of a program without having carefully analyzed the client's need. The client will use "understanding of the requirement" as a specific criterion item to be weighed and scored in evaluating technical proposals. Your strategy, then, is to present your understanding early in the proposal, and to do so in highly specific terms, as suggested in the proposal outline presented earlier.

Clarify the stated requirement, stripping away extraneous trivia that so often qualifies and clouds a client's statement of need, and, getting to the _essence_ of the requirement—define it. A true problem definition will at least suggest the solution or the next step toward a solution. For example, "inaccuracy of a tracking radar set that has been reported as being in good working order and with proper calibration procedures" is a symptom, but it is not the problem. The problem is probably inadequate training of users. Even that may be a symptom, with the real problem poor instruction practices or unqualified instructors. Or it may also be that the radar set is not in good working order at all, as represented in the RFP. The SOW included in the RFP may be in error, and you must consider this possibility also. The RFP may not define the problem, but only identify symptoms. While you may have to work to define the problem from what is stated in the RFP, that information also may suggest a worry item or a way to create one and a proposal strategy.

When the USPS issued an RFP calling for a "laundry list" of computer services in a call contract (Basic Ordering Agreement, that is), the need was stated as requiring the services of an organization that had on staff enough programmers and mixes of programming skills to enable the client to call for an almost infinite number of combinations of skills with a variety of computer languages, mainframe machines, and types of applications. It was a requirement that would have taxed, and might well have been beyond, the resources of even the largest computer services firms.

The successful proposer approached the problem by restating the requirement. He argued that it was not necessary for the contractor to have this vast pool of talent on staff, but only to be able to produce whatever programmers were called for when needed. He then demonstrated his company's ability and commitment to do this because it was a long-established supplier of "contract labor"—temporary technical writers, engineers, computer specialists, and other professionals and paraprofessionals. It even had a vast number of résumés on file in its own mainframe computer. The proposal specifically stated that the proposer regarded his proposal as completely responsive, despite a different approach to achieving the stated result, because the proposal satisfied the stated *need*, which, it stated, was the real test of responsiveness. The client obviously agreed with the argument by awarding the contract to that proposer.

Getting to the Negotiating Table

As a proposal consultant, I have had more than one client say to me, "You don't have to win the contract for me, and I don't expect you to. Just get me to the negotiating table, and I will take it from there."

That is a legitimate request, and I have always tried to do just that. Winning the contract is the end goal, of course, but getting to negotiate is a necessary intermediate step and so *it must be the direct objec-*

tive of writing the proposal, just as winning an interview ought to be the direct objective of writing and submitting a résumé.

The principle is that of addressing first things first or keeping your eye on the goal. Remember your end goal but remember you must reach your immediate objective before you can reach your goal. A job is not awarded directly to the writer of the most attractive proposal. Selection of best proposal(s) is only the first step. The next step is inviting the proposer(s) to the negotiation table. The client may include only the top proposer, the top five, or everyone whose proposal was acceptable. The invitation may be explained as an opportunity to submit a best and final offer (BAFO, in the jargon) or a meeting to "discuss" the proposal. In the case of small jobs, "getting to the table" or "negotiation" may be merely an informal telephone call to verify the stated contract terms to invite a BAFO by telephone or letter, or it may be a visit to the proposer by the contracting officer to verify the existence of a capability to do the work proposed.

Rarely is the term "negotiation" mentioned when a government client calls for a meeting after reading the proposal. Avoiding the word "negotiation" may be deliberate so that the proposer is not encouraged to believe that he or she is the favored contender and thus has a decided negotiating advantage. From the client's viewpoint, it is apparently much better negotiating strategy to keep the issue of contract award very much in doubt. Most often, the client wanted to "discuss" the proposal, asking questions and finally, after the discussions, asked me to document the answers I gave verbally at the table by now submitting them in a written amendment or addition to my proposal. That established, and the meeting concluding with the traditional thanks and handshakes, I would also be "invited," rather casually and at the last possible minute, almost as afterthought, to submit any changes to my cost figures that I might wish to present as my best and final offer. That was, in fact, probably one of the key objectives of the meeting, but the government contracting officials were often well trained in contract negotiations, often far more skilled in the art than were the proposers.

Benefits of Getting to the Table

Is there a good reason for getting to the table for any purpose other than contract negotiation? The client may invite you to meet for several possible reasons, such as:

- a standing policy to meet with all who submit acceptable proposals
- an interest in something provocative in your proposal and a desire to learn more about it
- a desire to get to know you for future procurements

There are several possible benefits in getting to the table with the client, even if the client does not yet have contract negotiation in mind. They are:

- You buy time, delaying an award decision while you do what you can to press your own suit for the contract.
- You make the client very much aware of your proposal so it will not be overlooked.
- Your credibility is greatly enhanced.
- You have the opportunity to make a presentation and do a selling job.

At the end of the meeting, you should have greatly strengthened your position in the competition. Certainly you will not be overlooked or forgotten as a contender for the contract.

Strategies for Getting to the Table

There are some situations that by their nature lend themselves to certain getting-to-the-table strategies. Weaknesses in the client's RFP—gaps in necessary information, for example—lay good groundwork for getting-to-the-table strategies.

Suppose, for example, that you raised some question in your proposal about important matters that were not covered in the RFP, but should have been. Can you persuade the client that these areas must be covered before any decisions are made about choosing a proposer for contract negotiations? Getting to the table only to clarify the client's need will get you noticed, will make the client fully aware of you and your proposal, and will give you a chance to talk to the client across the table and become known to her or him. It is automatically a significant boost to your chance of winning and, if handled well, almost always puts you up front in the competition.

What kinds of things can you say or do that will bring this result—that will induce in the client a sense of urgent need to talk to you before making an award decision? It is the raising of any concern that causes the client to suddenly suspect he is not yet ready to complete his evaluation or make even a tentative choice of one or more finalists in the proposal competition. Perhaps he has not thought through his need or problem enough, did not have enough information to issue a proper RFP, or does not have enough information now to make a wise choice. If your proposal can persuade the customer to reach any of these conclusions, the logical and usual reaction of the customer is to delay award decisions and seek more information—usually to ask you to visit and discuss these new concerns. (I will discuss how you get an exclusive hearing shortly.)

Offering an alternative proposal is one strategy that may bring this client reaction about if you can make a strong enough argument for the alternative. When the client's RFP does not furnish enough information for a properly definitive or truly responsive proposal, or, especially, to price the proposal, an alternative proposal may be in order.

I have been successful in using this strategy by pointing out the problem of pricing the project by listing the items normally needed for pricing. These have to be specified quantitatively and qualitatively. In the case of a requirement for writing and printing a report for an office of the Energy Department, for example, the RFP failed completely to provide quantitative specifications, necessary for pricing the writing and printing. We therefore offered a basic proposal, with our own suggested specifications for what we proposed as the minimum project configuration that would accomplish the client's objective, but we offered an alternative for a more sophisticated version. The client was somewhat stunned at how much needed information was not in the RFP. After he had been educated a bit by appropriate explanations in the proposal, he hastened to invite us to come in to discuss the project. (He admitted that he knew next to nothing about printing, and had not had any guidance in issuing the RFP.) We were able to use that meeting as a negotiating session and close the sale.

This kind of response in your proposal is part of educating the client, a frequently necessary element of your proposal, but one that requires a delicate touch. Your analysis must not come across as a criticism of the client's statement of need or disparagement of the client, but as a totally objective appraisal of needs and possible alternatives. Be helpful and help yourself to a contract.

As discussed in Chapter 1, making the client aware of deficiencies in the RFP may provoke a cancellation of the procurement. To minimize this possibility, avoid making any deficiency appear to be an excessively major fault, or even of mentioning any deficiency that does not advance a strategy you are developing. Even then, cancellation may be the result, but that is a necessary risk and not always a disadvantage. The client will often reissue the RFP with suitable revision, and you may well be in an advantageous position as a result of your earlier services to the client.

As discussed earlier, if it is all but impossible to be sure of the problem definition from the information in the RFP, this may create an opportunity to suggest to the client that preliminary work to analyze the project, validate the client's appraisal of the need, and make adjustments is necessary. This often suggests to the client a need to confer with you before proceeding to rewrite the RFP or award a contract.

When a client who developed training systems advised that their problem was that they never got a job out the door within either schedule or budget, we were forced to point out those were symptoms, and the problem could be with management decisions, procedures, competence of the staff, poor estimating, or some combination of these possibilities. An analysis was required to determine which it was, define the problem properly, and then design corrective action.

Here is another, more common example of a situation where the statement of the requirement leaves a good bit to be desired, and you can turn this to advantage in expediting an invitation from the client to confer. An RFP from the Federal Aviation Administration called for the creation of a report on the year's accomplishments of 22 various engineering offices of the FAA. It described a document to be printed in 500 copies by the contractor, containing an estimated 75 photos in color, and asking for an almost impossibly short schedule for the project.

Much was left unstated, such as who would provide the photos and what were the printing specifications for the report (paper, type fonts, covers, black and white or color printing, etc.), to name just a few undefined items that would greatly affect the effort and the costs, and might easily lead to serious contract disputes later if not defined in advance. (Earlier in this chapter I said I would tell you how to get an exclusive hearing with the client. Following are some examples.)

The successful proposer pointed out these and other problems, stressing the need to specify such things and the many hazards that could be encountered without such specification. To solve the problem without asking the client to furnish answers to the questions, he offered a primary proposal in which he offered specifications of all that needed to be specified and suggested that this was the minimum configuration that he thought necessary to satisfy the client's need. As an alternative, he offered a second set of specifications that would be a little more expensive, but would provide a somewhat more sophisticated and attractive product. He then submitted two separate cost proposals, one for each alternative. To answer a related question that I have often been asked, it is not necessary to create an entirely new and separate document as an alternative proposal. It is necessary to create only an additional chapter or section that clearly identifies itself as an alternative plan with an alternative set of specifications—and cost it with a separate cost form.

As he hoped and expected, this led directly to an invitation to visit the client and discuss the project and what was needed to get it started. That led to a brief negotiation and contract award.

Here is another example of a situation in which it was possible to induce the client to want to confer with you after reading your proposal. The client was the Product Safety Commission, and the project was to develop a number of safety manuals or pamphlets for the

Commission to print and distribute. The RFP suggested a few titles and subjects, and invited the proposers to offer their own suggestions.

The successful proposer did that, but went a step further: He suggested that he and the Commission establish a small team that would meet a few times to work together to brainstorm ideas for the publications. That so appealed to the client that they immediately invited the proposer to meet with them to discuss the idea. That soon grew into a contract negotiation and award.

This strategy of responding in such manner as to almost compel the client to invite you to discuss the requirement must be a part of your proposal so that it is presented to the client *after* and not *before* you have submitted your proposal. That timing is critical. If you raise the questions before the proposals are submitted, the client will respond in a way that no contender for the contract can complain of someone having the advantage of information not available to others. Those ways a client may respond to questions raised prematurely are these:

- Issue a response to your questions as a general memorandum to everyone who requested a copy of the RFP.
- Schedule a preproposal conference to discuss the questions. (Often, this is followed by mailing a report of the conference to all who were sent a copy of the RFP, so that any who did not attend the conference have no excuse for not being kept abreast of all developments that might otherwise represent a basis for protest.)
- Issue an amended RFP.
- Cancel the RFP, possibly to reissue it later.

None of these responses are in your interest, and you gain nothing from them. But if you raise the questions and furnish your own answers in your proposal, the client can negotiate with you independently and with no obligation to other proposers. This is what you want, of course, to "get to the table," while maintaining exclusivity to the ideas. It is another reason for not asking questions before proposals are submitted. You gain nothing that way, but you do gain a great advantage by answering your own questions in your proposal as part of your proposed program or as alternatives and options you offer the client.

This does not preclude a cancellation of the procurement. It is possible, even after proposals have been submitted, for the client to cancel the procurement so that he can amend the RFP and reissue it at a later date. You can reduce this risk if you are careful not to raise too many problems. In the case of the FAA requirement described in an earlier paragraph, there were other problems that the successful proposer did not mention, although his proposal would take care of them. It is best to focus on one serious problem that you can solve. Ignore the other problems, if they exist, to minimize the probability of provoking a cancellation by the client.

On the other hand, you can become the victim of your own ingenuity. This was the case in a proposal effort some years ago when the Communications and Weapons Division of the then Philco Corporation in Philadelphia prepared a proposal for the Defense Department in an effort to win a contract for a digital communications system. The RFP called for the provision of several mainframe computers as major components of the system. This proved to be a serious obstacle for the Philco engineering team, for reasons of no importance here. Already deep into the writing job, with many hours invested, the team was reluctant to abandon the proposal. Instead, they worked into the night devising an alternative plan, a more efficient way to get the job done without computers, by using several special digital devices that they would build. The client was so impressed with this plan, agreeing it was a much more efficient way to do the job, that it canceled the procurement and reissued the RFP, calling for a design sans computers! Of course, the engineering team knew that they risked cancellation, but could not find an alternative, other than abandoning the proposal effort. If they had been able to offer a responsive proposal, one that proposed the inclusion of the mainframe computers, they could have offered up the alternative later, after award, as an alternative plan. So there are two possible ways to handle such problems: offer up a radically different and better plan than the RFP suggests, or include the less-efficient plan that responds to the RFP and negotiate after getting the award.

In general, two considerations I mentioned earlier as elements of program quality that clients are likely to weigh seriously are (1) feasibility, and (2) innovative versus conservative ("tried and true") designs. Most of the opportunity for sales arguments in presenting your ideas to the client will occur in section II (in the proposal format offered earlier in this chapter), where you discuss the client's need and your approach for satisfying it. This is the groundwork for the specific plan you will describe, and it is here that you will or will not sell your approach and program. But do not overlook the importance of the subsection immediately preceding that, Understanding of the Requirement. Correctly identifying the true essence of what needs to be done is imperative to the credibility of your following analysis and discussion.

Just what will you sell in selling your plan? There are just two basic design *strategies*:

1. There is the comfortable and conservative approach of "how it's always done."
2. There is the dramatic and bold method of innovation, even to the extent of pushing the envelope.

There are, of course, degrees of "the tried and true," as there are degrees of boldness in design, but your design will probably appear to the client to fall into one or the other of these two classes of design strategy.

The conservative design approach is, of course, the familiar one, the one with minimal apparent risk and minimal noteworthiness. It has been in use for a long time, has been thoroughly debugged through long life, and offers great security with respect to design integrity. The innovative plan, on the other hand, commands attention, promises modernization and improvement over older designs, but being new and untried, also offers a degree of risk.

One slogan often heard in engineering that reflects this precise concern is "Evolution, not revolution." It's a slogan that says get to your goal in progressive steps, based on the known and reliable precedents already demonstrated, not in giant leaps. You can often sell bold advances in steps—evolutionary advances—but it is difficult to sell giant leaps based largely on speculative theory—revolution in design.

This does not mean that it cannot be done. Remember what you are selling in a proposal is a promise. You promise to produce a certain result, and you present your evidence of:

- Your understanding/appreciation of the requirement (section I)
- The rightness of your design (section II)
- The implementation of your design (section III)
- Your reliability and capability to carry the project out (section IV)

That is basic selling: It is promise of a result and proof (evidence) you can and will produce that result. Your proposal is intended to present the truth, but truth, for marketing purposes, is a perception of the client. If you wish to offer a bold design, you must work at assuring the client that it is not a risky one. Here is a case history, to illustrate at least one way a bold new innovation may be presented to make it attractive and yet not so bold as to be risky.

The client was an arm of the Postal Service, and the project was to develop a system for training maintenance technicians to be employed in a new kind of postal facility with much new mail-handling equipment.

Research showed that much of the equipment being bought was so new that most of it was prototype in nature. Models had worked in the laboratory, but they were still unknown quantities for daily use in a working environment. There was thus no maintenance history on most of it, and so proposers had to rely entirely on their own resources for designing a preventive maintenance system. The successful contender took a bold step in justifying the proposed program by the invention of a new system that he called "Failure Probability Analysis." It proved to be an effective USP. The new system was to overcome the lack of maintenance history on most of the system's components by assigning priorities of preventive maintenance on the basis of the analysis, which was to assign quantitative estimates of failure probability based on such factors as component population (number of similar components appearing in the establishment), experience with similar components, manufacturer's technical data, and criticality of the component. Those figures would establish a basis for specifying routine preventive maintenance, for weighting the training subjects, and also, as a bonus, provide data for estimating the required inventory of spare parts. (The latter information was a benefit beyond that required by the RFP, and so was a distinct extra selling point.)

The immediate problem was that the plan was probably too bold, on the face of it, and it would be criticized by conservative evaluators as untried and risky. To overcome this, the contender admitted quite frankly in his proposal that the system he had named Failure Probability Analysis was a new one, invented especially for this project. However, he pointed out, it was really not as radically new and different as a casual observer might assume, but was descended from a quite respectable background. It was the inverse of a well-established and widely accepted system of Reliability Analysis, which included such well-known measures as Mean Time Between Failures, which was one of the measures that Failure Probability Analysis would include. This argument, together with follow-up discussions with the client, overcame the client's uneasiness with a bold, new idea that was yet not really radical. The proposer got the contract.

In general, when offering something quite new and different, it is wise to work at making it appear far less revolutionary and more evolutionary. Give your bold, new ideas some respectability. Stress improvement, but do not stress differences as such. Proposals are no place for pioneering. Pioneers do not win contracts; they win arrows in their backs.

The Related Matter of Intelligence

In assessing a client's attitude toward bold and innovative designs versus conservative and well-established designs, proposal writers will often depend on verbal inputs from their sales managers who presumably know the customer well and have useful information. This is not always a reliable source. On at least one occasion, a proposer who was well-known to the customer and expected to submit the winning proposal lost the competition because the sales representative had been talking to an executive of the agency who disagreed with the purpose of the procurement and delivered his opinion as fact. Thus misled, the proposal writers offered an unacceptable plan. It is a good idea to treat all information, even that emanating from your own sources (especially verbal information), with a touch of skepticism until you can confirm it somehow.

There is yet more, much more, to consider in the matter of presentation and writing strategies, and for that we go on to a fresh chapter.

Presentation Strategies: II

8

How Many Presentation Strategies Are There?

There are a number of aspects to your presentation strategy. First, there is the impact of your physical presentation—your proposal. Perhaps we should say strategies since, for a printed proposal alone, several matters are covered: the cover, illustrations, typography, and other factors of physical appearance. Any ancillary presentations are also strategies, such as oversize originals of key illustrations (a major flowchart, for example), photographs, videotapes, audiotapes, or other aids to the presentation. There also are other considerations of presentation such as arranging information for maximum impact, including narrative "hooks," optimum order of presentation (e.g., building to an attention-getting climax), development of key words, and organization in general. Overall, presentation strategy includes both the physical impact of the proposal and the emotional/rational impact of the idea development presented by the text.

Both are considerations in the suggested proposal format for specific sections or chapters, but each section is based on its own general strategy as an element of the presentation strategy overall. The text ought to present a road map to guide the reader's thinking to the climax and conclusions desired by the proposer. Thus, it is necessary to define a role for each section of the proposal and understand where it fits into the general scheme of presentation strategy.

The Technical Discussion

The last element of the introduction, according to the recommended outline and format presented in Chapter 7, should have described your understanding of the requirement in its essence, expressed in your own words, independently and distinctly different from the words used in the RFP. Two reasons for using entirely different language in stating your understanding of what the customer needs are:

1. Reading a differently expressed view of the requirement, based on someone else's impressions and conclusions, is likely to be an enlightenment for the customer. Certainly, it helps greatly to assure the customer that you have analyzed the requirement and drawn your own independent conclusions therefrom about the client's needs. In fact, in a great many cases "understanding of the requirement" is a point of evaluation by which technical proposals will be judged and scored. Failure to clearly state the client's requirements will be cause for rejecting the proposal as nonresponsive.

2. On the other hand, we humans sometimes mistakenly adopt an idea as our own opinion, because we have not really thought through the matter. But when you compel yourself to find completely different language—including different analogies, examples, or other imagery—you are forced to truly *think* about the subject. Sometimes you discover that you do not agree with the conclusions of needs drawn by those who wrote the RFP. In fact, your ability to explain the client's requirement in totally different (preferably lay) language is itself an acid test of your understanding. If you are having difficulty in making this translation, perhaps you do not understand the requirement.

It is always possible that when you study the RFP closely, you will not agree with the customer's analysis and description of need, and you will have to somehow express that objectively in your summation. It is also possible that as you develop the program, you discover that you now have come to some disagreement with what the RFP had to say. In either case, the words you use there are the introduction (and bridge) to the next section of your proposal, the extended discussion of the client's requirement. The understanding of the requirement that you express in the first section must be parallel with the technical discussion that it introduces as the subject of the second section. It is entirely possible that as you write and develop the technical discussions and explanations, you will find that you are really still developing the program design, still analyzing the problem, and still synthesizing the solution or "thinking on paper," as one colleague of mine expressed it.

This technical discussion section is a most important part of your proposal because it is where you present the bulk of your sales arguments. Here, you introduce the most important section of your proposal, the program you propose, and where you work at helping the customer see why this is by far the best plan and you are the best candidate for carrying it out.

Strategy for This Section

This second section is a technical discussion, even if the subject is not a technological requirement. It is technical in the sense that among the things you must demonstrate here are your knowledge of and capability for designing and carrying out a solution for the customer's problem. You must show here the knowledge of the work skills and crafts required, whether the project is one that requires knowledge and experience in accounting, office procedures, sign making, construction, training, warehouse management, or any other field that is not highly technological. Remember: You are writing a proposal because the customer requires custom work to provide products or services that cannot be bought off the shelf. This means that you must create a custom program of some sort to satisfy the need. The discussion here is therefore technical in the sense that you must explain your analysis of the need in extended terms, what it takes to satisfy it, how you propose to do so—the project or program you propose—and why this is the best and perhaps only sensible way to go.

There are almost always several ways to address and approach any problem, and you will want to explain or at least point out each of these, describe and discuss the pros and cons of each possible option, identify and explain the approach you have chosen, and present your rationale for opting for that approach. Here you must use both emotion and reason, benefit and logic. This is the section where you can address or create and address a worry item (using fear motivation). You can talk about the skills needed to bring about a good solution (possibly a competitive strategy). You can discuss new ideas of your own, explain that special item or special benefit you promised earlier (gain motivation), bring in your big surprise, promise that you will offer both a completely responsive program and an alternative you think to be a better choice (if such is the case), and otherwise unleash the big guns of your sales argument. This is the chief selling ground. Although there are other opportunities to make important selling points, this is the place to present your chief sales arguments, explaining why the approach you have chosen produces the greatest benefits, involves the lowest risks, or otherwise is the best choice. If you can make a reasonable case that will show all other approaches to be risky, by all means do so. Fear motivation, when justified, often is far more persuasive than is gain motivation.

This section should then culminate in the summing up of the approach you have chosen to use. It will then serve as an introduction and bridge to the next section, which is the proposal proper: the chapter and verse of your proposal, qualified and quantified descriptions, and schedules of precisely what you promise to do and guarantee to achieve.

The Proposed Project

Strategy for This Section

The third section of your proposal is a place for objective, declaratory statements. This section is the actual proposal, your specific offer.

It is a place to lay out the details of your proposed program. And that offers an opportunity of its own for an effective strategy. The more details you present here, the better your chances for being invited to sit down and discuss your proposal. There are at least two excellent reasons for this:

1. The more specific and objectively presented details you offer, the more persuasive is your presentation. It is easy enough to generalize about almost anything under the sun and present an armful of credentials, but it takes more than that to achieve credibility. When you can explain your program in detail, especially in *quantified* detail, you give evidence that you have done your homework, that you know your field, and that you know what you are talking about.

2. The more specific and detailed the information you present about your program, the more easily understandable the presentation of your program becomes, and the more the customer can and probably will identify with it. That wealth of detail in your presentation invites and inspires the customer to analyze and think about your program and develop questions about its elements, as you have listed and described them. You want the customer to know as much about the proposed program in all its details, even to disagree with some of what you present. It encourages the customer to become *involved* psychologically with your proposed program. This, in turn, becomes an influence that helps induce an invitation to visit and discuss your proposal.

It should therefore come as no surprise that the proposal philosophy here encourages you to provide as much detailed and objective information—facts, not opinions or generalizations—as possible, and to quantify it as well as qualify it.

Facts versus Sales Arguments

There are no sales arguments per se called for or appropriate to this third section of your proposal, except as may be implied by the simple facts you present here or what is inferred by the customer. This is the section of your proposal that should be entirely factual in tone and language. It is where you describe your program in objective detail: what you will do, how you will do it, how much of it you will do, and perhaps what the customer must do, such as make reviews and comment, according to some schedule. (More on the latter subject shortly, in discussing deliverables and schedules.) But there is a special significance to this section of your proposal. In the interest of efficiency and reducing the amount of paperwork, the government has long included the selected proposal in the contract by reference. In actuality, it is this section that describes specifics of schedule and products of the technical proposal (and the cost proposal) that is the significant element of the contract, the exhibit, the statement of what you agree to do and the customer accepts as the basis for the contract. This explains why, at the conclusion of a "discussion" or BAFO, you are asked to submit to the contracting office a written amendment to your proposal documenting all changes and points to which you have agreed. You have actually been negotiating contract provisions, and they must now be documented in writing to become part of the contract that is (presumably) soon to be signed.

The fact that you do not present sales arguments per se in this section does not preclude including material here to support sales arguments you made in earlier sections of the proposal. In fact, that ought to be a major concern and one major objective of this third section of your proposal. The second and third sections of your proposal are directly analogous to the "proof and promise" concept of advertising/sales technique. The first and second sections—especially the second one—offered the promises, and the third section offers the proof (although the fourth section of your proposal will also make its contributions here) by explaining how the promises will be made good by your program. Consider the opportunities here to support your sales arguments in this way.

Project Management

Management is always a concern of customers, and in some cases it is such a major concern that it needs to have a chapter or section of its own (even a separate volume, in some truly large proposals) for extended discussion. For simplicity here, we will assume that management may be included as a first element of the third section of your proposal. Here, in describing your proposed management methods and procedures, you may find it a good strategy to name your proposed project manager and even other senior staff members of the proposed project. In some cases, you can provide a brief introduction of the individual, with the chief qualifications of each that are most relevant to the project, and explain that résumés will appear later. If any such individual, especially the head of the project, has some extra-strong qualifications of any kind, such as recent successful management of a similar program or some unusual but relevant experience or skill, this is an excellent place to make that point by presenting this experience or skill as simple fact, without comment. But describe here all your excellent management methods, forms, controls, liaison with the customer, and other evidence that your management plan is comprehensive, meticulous, and foolproof. This is where you strive to make the customer feel good, comfortable, and safe in your hands.

Here, it may also help greatly to bring in a hint of what will appear in the next section—information about your organization generally—by showing the linking of proposed project management with organization management in general via a reporting order that keeps your organization management well posted at all times on the project, and demonstrates their interest in the success of the project. All customers want to be assured that their work is important to you, and this is a way to express an appreciation of your concern for the complete satisfaction of the customer's need.

Here, too, you may make good use of the idea introduced in Chapter 1 of the three-track functional flowchart. Supply one or more full-size (suitable for mounting on an office wall) charts as an exhibit or appendix to the proposal. Preferably make it something that is of direct usefulness to the customer, either in facilitating understanding of your proposal or in the customer's management of matters pertaining to the project. That idea may be adapted to and used effectively in many situations and applications. One variation on that idea is the inclusion in the proposal of a special kind of status or management chart. The chart will enable the customer's project manager to keep track of project progress, be alerted to important dates in the schedule, and otherwise monitor the project and report to his or her own management on its progress. The chart designed for use by the customer's project manager may be prepared on some suitable art board in a size suitable for mounting on the wall of an office—maybe three by four feet—where it may be used effectively, while also available for viewing as a continually up-to-date status report. (The chart would include schedule dates, milestones, and other key data.) Experience has been that customers are impressed by this idea. And, of course, the chart helps evaluators follow the strategies of the program design as they read and evaluate the proposal itself, a beneficial side effect. (As a practical measure, the chart may be prepared originally in that form, and then page-size copies can be made to include in the proposal, while the original is covered with a clear acetate sheet on which grease-pencil checks and notations may be made.)

Be sure to alert the client to the chart(s) existence and purpose. And for maximum effectiveness, package the chart and proposal together for delivery. A three-by-five-foot proposal gets attention, especially since it cannot be put on the shelf, along with other proposals submitted, but must be stored in some more prominent position. Mark the outer wrapping boldly to ensure that there is no doubt that the package is a proposal by stating in large characters something such as "Proposal Response to RFP No. _____."

In some cases, the customer expresses concern in an RFP about administrative management of the contract, often asking specifically who the customer's contracting officer should call, if need be, to discuss the contract or related matters, such as invoices and expenses. But even if there is no mention of this in the RFP, it may be helpful to your overall strategy to make mention of contract liaison with the customer's contracting officer by the responsible individual in your organization.

A word of caution about liaison: Some customers show concern about how the customer's project manager will interface with your project manager and be kept informed. In government contracts, the project manager may be known as the Contracting Officer's Representative (COR) or Contracting Officer's Technical Representative (COTR). Some overeager proposal writers propose so much and such continuous liaison with the COTR that the customer has been inspired to say something such as, "Are you asking us to manage this project for you?" Offer a passive reporting system—periodic written reports are the usual practice—but provide for special reports or alerts when and if a problem arises that threatens the progress or success of the program. Customers usually think it important that they be notified immediately of serious problems, but they vary in how much liaison they want. A busy customer may want minimal involvement—other than regular progress reports, whereas another customer may want to be kept closely informed at all times.

Labor Loading Estimates and Charting

Labor loading is a process that identifies the phases, functions, and activities of the project you propose, and estimates just how much labor is required for each, who of your project staff will do those things, and how long each will take (see Figure 8.1). Many contracts are labor-intensive, making labor loading a major element in both cost estimating and explanation of phases and functions to be carried out. In the typical case, the chart will usually be much longer and even more complex, with many more tasks and subtasks than those shown in the simple example here. It can become invaluable both as a focal point for negotiation and as a strong support of your sales strategy. In fact, developing these analyses and estimates as a chart does several things for you:

1. A labor loading chart is an important support for your cost proposal, especially when the project is a labor-intensive one— when the bulk of the expense you incur is for labor. It demonstrates to the customer a sound basis for your costs, and shows the customer as specifically as possible where, what, and how much effort is required.

Figure **8.1**	Labor Loading Estimates

Staffing and Hours

Tasks	No. of Project Managers	No. of Senior Engineers	No. of Junior Managers	Technicians
1. Meeting with COTR	8	8	16	—
2. Prepare preliminary design specs	24	40	40	40
3. Review with COTR	16	16	—	—
4. Breadboard circuit	24	40	80	40
5. Test breadboard	—	12	24	24
6. Build prototype		12	24	40
7. Test prototype				
a. Lab	—	12	24	24
b. Field	8	8	24	24
TOTALS:	80	148	232	192

2. It supports your functional flowchart and schedules, and should track with and validate them. It also supports your sales arguments because specific details are believable where generalizations are suspect.

3. It supports your cost estimates and should track with and validate estimated costs.

4. It is an aid in making your cost estimates, or an alternative method for estimating costs, and helps you develop confidence in the cost estimates if the labor loading tracks well with the estimates, but alerts you to the need for close checking if it does not track well with them.

5. It is a valuable aid in negotiations, furnishing a basis for bargaining with the customer over the details of the tasks, staff levels, and labor required for each task. The more specific the items that are the subject of bargaining, the more likely it is that you will reach agreement. One of the valuable assets of this bargaining tool is that you can reduce costs, when necessary to close the contract, by eliminating or reducing some of the tasks and labor.

You can use an analysis of tasks and labor such as this to arrive at your cost estimates, or you may use this kind of analysis as a check on the cost estimates you have developed by some other method. (I never have complete confidence in my cost estimates until I have developed the labor loading estimates and priced them.)

Deliverable Items

There should always be at least one deliverable item. At the minimum, it will be a report or other document, on paper or perhaps on a computer disk. Let us assume here that there will be several end-items resulting from the work to be delivered to the customer. Many contractors describe the deliverables, but fail to specify them, and there is a substantial difference. Describing the item is a qualification, but a full specification requires quantifying information—how heavy, how wide, how tall, how many, and other such information.

Both kinds of specification are important to avoid disputes later. Surprisingly often, there was a lack of full specification. The customer did not provide a close specification of the work, especially the deliverables, in writing the RFP, and the contractor likewise failed to offer a full specification in responding to the RFP. The contractor evidently assumes, in such cases, that the customer will accept whatever the contractor delivers and believes to be suitable, since the contractor is the expert. This is a mistaken assumption, of course, and the basis for future trouble. The customer may very well interpret the loose wording or the lack of wording however he or she chooses, and the customers understandably choose to interpret the contract in some way favorable to them and not to the contractors. In disputes arising as a consequence of this carelessness, the contractor almost always loses. The contract is only as tight, binding, and protective of your interests as the specifications it includes. Failing to specify what you will deliver for the price you place on your services is writing a blank check, defeating the purpose in writing a contract.

For example, in one case, the customer, which happens to have been the Bureau of Naval Personnel, asked for a manual to be written on a military subject, and asked for the manual to be well illustrated with line drawings as graphic examples, but did not specify the number of pages nor the number of illustrations. Fortunately, this contractor furnished his own specifications of what he believed to be suitable and proposed to deliver, and specified how many pages and how many illustrations he would provide, as he described the manual that was the required deliverable item.

The customer's project manager liked what he got as a final product, but now thought that the product should have more pages and more illustrations, and so requested them of the contractor. The contractor refused to do so, unless the customer would accept and pay for a suitable contract amendment providing more funds. The matter went to the agency's contracting official as a dispute.

The contract was carefully reviewed, with special attention to the specifications provided by the contractor in the proposal. With all the facts presented, the contracting official finally turned to the project manager and asked, "Do you have money to pay for more than you originally contracted for?"

The project manager admitted that he had no further funds in his budget. At that, the contracting official pronounced the contract completed and ruled in favor of the contractor's position.

Not all such disputes end so favorably for the contractor. Almost inevitably, when true specifications are not provided by either party, the contractor is obliged to surrender to the customer's demands or at least reach a compromise, unreasonable although either result may be. Even if the contractor prevails, there has been a dispute that can delay payment for a long time and may become bitter enough to cause enmity and the loss of future business. Specify deliverable items completely in your proposal. You are writing what is to be an essential part of a contract. If you are successful, you are making a contractual commitment. You can then be calm and businesslike in handling demands or disputes.

Important as these considerations are, even from the viewpoint of sales strategy, precise specification is important to credibility. Quantifying refers to specification, not to statistics. "Several thousand" or even "more than 10,000" is unacceptable. Use precise figures, such as 10,175. The latter is accepted by a reader as fact; the former expressions are smoke. Even when you arrive at some quantity by estimate, report the precise number; do not round it off, if you want your number to be accepted without skepticism.

Schedules

Schedules are another place where you can inadvertently lay the groundwork for a dispute by not being specific. This is especially the case when the schedule involves, and is even partially dependent on, some interaction with the customer.

One problem that arises with schedules is caused by a lack of clarity in definition. Here is a typical schedule that you might encounter in an RFP for a small contract to write a manual:

Task/Subtask	*Due*
Draft book plan	10 DAA (Days After Award)
Customer review, comments	20 DAA
Revised book plan	30 DAA
Draft manuscript	90 DAA
Customer review, comments	20 DAA
Revised manuscript	150 DAA
Customer review, comments	180 DAA
Final delivery of camera-ready copy	210 DAA

There are two problems with this schedule. The first one is that "days" are not defined. Are they calendar days or working days? There is almost a 30-percent difference in time between the two. That's ample "opportunity" for a dispute and serious conflict. Specify which kind of day is meant.

There is another potential for a future problem apparent here in the matter of customer review. More often than not, the customer does not complete the review in the time allotted in such a schedule. That throws the timetable off completely, of course, and all too often the customer expects the contractor to make up the lost time somehow.

One immediate remedy is to make such changes in the schedule as those in the following example:

Task/Subtask	*Due*
Draft book plan	10 Working days after award
Customer review, comments	20 Working days after award
Revised book plan	10 Working days after customer review

Draft manuscript	30	Working days after customer review
Customer review, comments	60	Working days after customer review
Revised manuscript	30	Working days after customer review
Customer review, comments	30	Working days after customer review
Final delivery of camera-ready copy	30	Working days after customer review

This, of course, automatically requires the customer to allow any schedule extensions made necessary by the customer's delay in meeting schedule dates. It greatly reduces the possibility of disputes because the customer has agreed to this schedule in accepting your proposal and making it an exhibit to the contract. In general, disputes can be avoided, or at least minimized, by great care in specifying all deliverables, goods, and services, as precisely as possible in quantitative, as well as qualitative terms. (In fact, precise quantitative specifications are much easier to arrive at, usually, than qualitative ones, and it is difficult for anyone to misinterpret numbers expressed precisely.)

Résumés

The last part of this section of your proposal is a good place for the résumés of your proposed project principals. (It is not ordinarily necessary to provide résumés of other project personnel, such as clerical and administrative workers.) Then, if you want to include résumés of other qualified personnel as evidence of your organization's capability, you may include those in the next section or in an appendix, so there is no confusion about who is to be assigned to the project.

The format most useful for a résumé in this application need not resemble the format most commonly used for a résumé sent to prospective employers in a job-seeking campaign. It is neither necessary nor desirable to offer a great deal of detailed information about the individual's history. What is needed here is only a summary of the individual's background, revealing principal qualifications and credentials of training, experience, and achievements. A résumé should not normally require more than one page, and when space is limited, it can usually be done in a half page.

Each résumé should carry an indication of the individual's regular position and title in the organization, and the position and title he or she will have in the proposed program. The latter position/title obviously will change with each new project, and the former usually will change from time to time in one's career, even a career spent in a single organization.

To further this system, a flexible résumé format should be designed. Figure 8.2 shows a suggested general format. A model, using the suggested format, is presented as Figure 8.3.

Using Consultants or Contract Labor

It is not uncommon to require the services of a specialist to handle a project responsibility for which no regular member of your staff is well qualified. In such case, you would normally retain a consultant or find a suitable candidate for temporary or permanent employment if

Figure 8.2	Suggested General Résumé Format

Name
Position in the Proposing Organization
Position in Proposed Project

Summary paragraph(s) of most relevant education, experience, training, and achievements relevant to proposed project.
Supporting information relevant and important to the proposed project, but of secondary importance.

| Figure 8.3 | A Sample Résumé |

Harold W. Martin, Ph.D.
Communications Engineer, Accurate Electronics
PRINCIPAL INVESTIGATOR
Capricorn Research Project

Dr. Martin is a magna cum laude graduate of the Massachusetts Institute of Technology, where he taught physics for several years before joining the staff of Accurate Electronics. He has been with Accurate Electronics for 14 years, the past six in charge of communications systems development.

Dr. Martin has had direct responsibility recently for the development of special components of secure communications systems for NASA and the United States Air Force, to be used in various satellite, logistics, and command systems, earning special commendations for Accurate Electronics from both agencies as a result of his work.

Dr. Martin's work at Accurate Electronics has involved a great deal of research and development activity. He has proved to be a highly creative engineer, and holds 11 patents for special communications devices, all assigned to Accurate Electronics and developed over the past six years.

He will be assigned to the proposed Capricorn Research Project as the Principal Investigator, devoting his full time to that work.

and when the contract were awarded to you. Where the proposed position to be filled by that individual is an important one, you will need to include the résumé of that individual.

A problem can arise in that connection. It is normally months later before a contract is awarded and work can begin. The implication of including that résumé without comment is that the individual is a current employee. Or, if you indicate otherwise, the customer will probably want some assurance that you are not simply "hanging paper," the practice of some proposers to include résumés of individuals who do not even know that their résumés are in your hands—much less that their employment on a project has been promised. More specifically, the customer will want to know what assurance you can offer that the individual will, in fact, be available for the assignment. It is therefore an excellent idea to avoid hanging paper and to get a letter from the individual assuring you that he or she agrees to employment for the project and pledges to be available for it. A copy of that letter or a statement that such a letter exists should be included with the résumé. Otherwise, you run the risk of being embarrassed and having your credibility greatly reduced by failure to produce guarantees when asked for them. In fact, even the necessity to admit that an individual for whom a résumé is included is not a current employee is harmful, and it is best to be completely frank about this up front, where it will probably draw no special attention in any form.

Not having everyone you need on your immediate staff is not a weakness in your proposal unless you permit it to be a weakness. On the contrary, you can make it a plus—a great strength, in fact. (This is a general rule to be followed for any and all cases where you think you have some weakness to overcome. Never sound apologetic, but always turn that perceived weakness into a strength.) You can handle the presentation of a proposed consultant or prospective new employee in this manner: explain that some special skill or talent is required for one of the important project functions, and while your own staff could do the job, you believe that the requirement merits a true specialist in that function for best results. You are pleased to report that, with a great deal of effort, you were successful in finding just the right specialist for this function and to arrange for him or her to guarantee to be available for the project. You might, in fact, want to plant the seeds of this idea earlier, in the technical discussion of the project.

Proposer's Qualifications

This fourth section of the suggested proposal format is your company's résumé, tailored to whatever are the special needs of the proposal. Normally included here are a description of your overall business organization, your principals, facilities and resources, and record of achievements. (In fact, the RFP may specifically request a record of the latter.) You also may find it advantageous to include in this section additional résumés of senior people on your permanent staff.

Strategy for This Section

Given three things to prove—a program that is persuasive as a viable and effective solution for the customer's problem, a suitable capability for carrying out the program, and reliability as a contractor—this section focuses primarily on the second and third of these three qualities. The earlier elements of the proposal should have focused on demonstrating the existence of the first element and made a major contribution to demonstrating the second (capability) as well. The strategy for this section is, therefore, obvious. It will demonstrate and prove—beyond any and all doubts—both your capability and reliability for carrying out the proposed program successfully. Following are the distinct items to offer in presenting that proof, with explanations of substrategies, as appropriate.

The Overall Organization

- Name your organization, using its full and formal name, and explain the nature of the organization as a sole proprietorship, partnership, or corporation. Describe pertinent history:
  - Founding of the organization and special circumstances surrounding that founding, if they are of interest.
  - The general business/activity/interests of the organization.
  - The basic resources and facilities: physical plant, divisions, financial resources. (The latter is often of special interest to contracting officials when the contract is a sizable one and will require substantial amounts of operating capital.
- Name your principals—president, vice presidents, and senior managers, preferably with a word or two about each.

- Offer a simple organizational chart to demonstrate how you are organized functionally, where/how the proposed project will fit in the overall organization, and to whom (what office or individual) the project manager will report. A substrategy is in effect here: Customers want you to take them and their needs quite seriously, and you must make it clear here that they and their business are important to you. Therefore, appoint as senior a person as possible to manage the project and show that individual reporting as high in the organization as possible. For a large project, it is appropriate to construct a special organization chart for this purpose to dramatize the importance of the project and the authority of its manager.
  - Customers want to be assured that your project manager has authority to make commitments to the customer's project manager and act promptly (i.e., that your project manager will not have to report to some committee or higher authority for approval of even minor decisions). It is a good idea to be quite specific about this and show the reporting order as one of keeping higher management *informed,* rather than of getting approval of every action required.
- Furnish direct evidence of your track record. Often, the customer will specifically request that you report recent contracts similar to that for which you are proposing, with information on how your performance met the schedule dates and was completed within the budget, and the names and telephone numbers of those who can confirm your representations in this regard. This should be a tabular presentation, laying out the data as prescribed. It is not necessary to list all contracts, but only a few that will show the relevance of your experience and capability, and your reliability as a contractor. There is also no particular order in which these must be presented. Start with the most appropriate (most favorable) one, and add a few until you have made your point. Indicate that there are many others and that you will present them, if desired. (They rarely are called for if you have presented five or six good records with complete data.) But even if such data is not specifically requested in the

RFP, you may furnish it voluntarily, and it is usually a plus to do so.

- List any special facilities or resources you own or have special access to and which may have some bearing on the work proposed such as laboratories, field offices, or subsidiaries. (Perhaps, for example, you have a field office close by the customer's location, and you can offer to do or headquarter the work there. Customers often prefer to have their projects in work near their own facilities.)
- This is a place to also post information about any special awards, patents, letters of commendation, and other testimonials to the organization's achievements. (If you do not have letters of commendation from customers, it is because you did not think to ask for them. Unfortunately, most customers do not think to write such letters unless they are prompted to do so, but a satisfied customer usually will agree to furnish such letters.)
- Finally, this is a place to post brief résumés of other senior people in the organization to reinforce your image of capability and to demonstrate that you have ample numbers of qualified personnel to back up those proposed for assignment to the project. In some cases, the number and quality of résumés provided is an influential factor in evaluation of your proposal.

This, then, covers the main body of the proposal, but there is much more that can be provided, primarily in front matter, that can contribute substantially to the success of your proposal. Chapter 9 will help you make the most of this opportunity.

9

Front Matter and Back Matter

Proposal Front Matter and Sales Strategies

Sales strategy and the opportunities to contribute to sales strategy are not confined to any one area of your proposal, as must now be clear. Almost every portion of your proposal can be designed and executed in some manner that supports the overall objective of the proposal: winning the contract.

As a formal document, your proposal is normally bound with a number of elements that appear before the introductory chapter of your proposal. Collectively, these are known as front matter, and were listed in Chapter 7 in the outline of a suggested proposal format. They offer their own excellent opportunities to add weight to your sales arguments.

Five items were listed earlier as front matter that should be considered as factors in the strategies of proposal success. They follow the title page and precede the first section or chapter of your proposal. The normal sequence of the items are:

1. Copy of letter of transmittal
2. Foreword or preface
3. Table of contents
4. Executive summary
5. Conformance or response matrix

Despite this normal sequence of appearance in a proposal, discussion of these elements is another matter, and for logical continuity of explanation, we will start with a brief word about the foreword or preface.

Foreword or Preface

There are cases where a foreword is useful in a proposal because you have some information or idea to present that does not fit comfortably into any other section. For this reason, it is listed as a possible element of front matter. The executive summary—and to some extent the introductory chapter of your proposal—present much the same points as would a preface or foreword, although they are not interchangeable. The inclusion of an executive summary, which I highly recommend, therefore makes a foreword redundant.

The Executive Summary

A well-executed executive summary is a powerful sales tool. Its nominal purpose is to present an abstract of the proposal for the customer's top-level managers and officials, who would not normally read the entire proposal. It is thus written in lay terms, as much as possible, with technical jargon defined when it must be used.

Strategy for the Executive Summary

Although the executive summary is nominally an abstract of the proposal intended to brief busy executives, in practice it is generally also used to sell the project. Well used, it can be a primary sales tool. (That is, with major focus on the major selling points.) Although the executive summary is intended for those who will not read the full proposal, with all its details, it is inevitable that anyone who has an interest in the project, including those whose responsibility it is to evaluate and grade the proposal, will read the executive summary before they read any other part of the proposal.

Figure	
9.1	**A Portion of a Typical Executive Summary**

Executive Summary

Following are the highlights and main points of the proposal presented here, offering to install a highly professional system for the management and administration of a third-party claims service for the Client County and Client self-insurance program, and describing a multiplicity of important benefits offered:

1. Blank & Co. are thoroughly experienced in providing third-party claims services to insurance companies, governments, and others, such as the Client division of Client organization.

2. We will install an Instant Response System (IRS) to be manned and operated in its entirety (equipment and staff) in Client County, Main at Second Streets, with corporate backup support in nearby (town).

3. The software used in the system will be, in effect, special and exclusive to Client County's self-insurance program because it will be the proposer's proprietary software, which we have already redesigned and customized especially to the needs of this program, as described in the RFP.

4. The system will provide instant response, initiating claim files, assigning unique claim file numbers, and updating the database accordingly, immediately and spontaneously, as claim data is received, whether by telephone, mail, or hand delivery.

5. The entire system will be dedicated to—used exclusively for—third party claims service for the Client County self-insurance program. Client County data will never have to wait in line for access to a computer handling other people's programs nor run the hazard of having the Client database corrupted by data that belongs in other files.

6. All data entered will be immediately available to authorized Client personnel via remote viewing on screen and/or downloading of files. (Viewing and downloading may be to Client mainframe, mini-, desktop, or portable computers.)

Therefore, the summary is so organized as to present and stress the principal selling points of the proposal. Figure 9.1 displays an exemplary portion of one such summary used in a proposal to a county government. (The proposer is represented as "Blank" and the client as "Client" to respect the individual's and organization's privacy.)

Without knowledge of the subject and of the Statement of Work that appeared in the RFP, the sales appeal and strategies of the individual items listed are not apparent here. They were pointed at what the proposer was clearly implying were shortcomings and disadvantages in the county's existing program, as it had been described in the RFP and according to what the proposer knew of such programs and systems. Every one of the 14 points included in the two-page executive summary was so constructed and designed to highlight the benefits of what the proposed system would *do* for the county government and for the officials responsible for its programs, while summarizing the system proposed.

Thus, the executive summary is a miniproposal, translating any technical detail into explanations in lay language.

Copy of Letter of Transmittal

It is customary to address a proposal to the individual signing the letter that accompanies and presents the RFP or to whomever the RFP designates as the proper recipient of the proposal requested. In governments, this would normally be a contracting official. There are marketers who believe that a letter of transmittal sent with a proposal submittal is an unimportant, routine document that does little but state a proposal is hereby presented. Possibly this view is prompted by the thought that the contracting official has little to do with evaluating technical proposals and choosing one as the best. There are others who believe the letter of transmittal is the most important element of the response to the RFP. Opinions vary widely, and perhaps both are valid, to a limited extent, depending on individual cases where circumstances vary widely.

For the general case, probably the truth falls somewhere between those extremes. Whatever the case, because it must be included, do not throw away the opportunity to sell.

Strategy for the Letter of Transmittal

Several government contracting officers, asked about their immediate interest in proposals, have told me that their first interest is "how much"—the cost, that is. They are not concerned about technical content because that evaluation is assigned to a technical selection team. But by instinct and training (contracting officers tend to be lawyers or accountants, and many are both), they tend to look at costs and to be interested in the proposal offering the lowest cost. Accordingly, a letter of transmittal can be designed to enlist the contracting officer's support by stating the cost of the proposed project and summarizing your attitude toward and provisions for cost control. If you have some special system or program to manage costs and keep them to a minimum, mention of that may be made in the letter, with reference to its coverage in the proposal.

This may make the letter of transmittal somewhat redundant with the executive summary, but that is not a negative factor, since the two elements are intended for different readers. However, strategically, it is a good idea to express the coverage in a different manner in the letter of transmittal.

There is one problem with doing this. If your letter of transmittal stated the bottom-line price of the project, it is ordinarily a no-no to include cost information in the technical proposal. The way to handle this problem is to organize the letter of transmittal in such a way as to make it easy to delete the price information from the copy of the letter that is bound into the proposal. (The original copy is in an ordinary business envelope addressed to the contracting officer and accompanies the proposal package.) One way to do this is to state the cost information separately at the top right-hand corner of the letter. It is then easy to block this information out when copying the original. Another way is to state the costs on an enclosure with the letter that goes with only the original letter. Of course, the contracting official may also open the cost proposal, a separate document in the case of government procurements, but learning the cost from the letter of transmittal is a convenience for the contracting officer.

Although including prices in the technical proposal is banned, there is no reason to withhold discussions of cost control goals and measures, so the rest of the letter of transmittal is an acceptable element of the proposal, and proposal reviewers should also be interested in your proposed cost management. In some cases, this is listed in an RFP as a specific proposal element to be judged and included in the evaluation.

Table of Contents

Many proposal writers use a spartan table of contents, one which lists only the chapter or section heads and their page numbers. But there is nothing to prevent you from listing all the heads, at least those of the first order, but preferably including even those of a second order, plus a list of all illustrations, tables, or other nonverbal content. So designed, the table of contents acts as an outline of the proposal, and even as an index. But it can do more than that, too. Even a table of contents can have a strategic value of its own in the overall proposal sales strategy.

Strategy for the Table of Contents

The point was made earlier in a number of places, such as in Chapter 7, under the subsection Proposal Formats, that every heading and caption should be chosen to help present sales arguments. So instead of writing "Introduction" as the title of an introductory paragraph, you might write something such as was reported earlier that one proposal writer wrote, "A New Broom," to introduce the argument that the proposer would bring a fresh view to the project. Or a discussion might be introduced with, "The New and Different Ideas Henry & Company Will Introduce."

If this is done assiduously, the resulting table of contents presents a series of sales arguments. And if the same writing philosophy is followed as that recommended for the writing of the introductory chapter of the proposal, you will build the table of contents as you go, rather than assembling at the end. By so doing, you will have the opportunity to scan the growing list of heads and subheads, and be sure that they follow some logical sequence and pattern. Or you can go back and change some of them to enhance the overall pattern. If you find some logical gaps in the sequence as it appears in the table of contents, you can return to that section of the proposal and insert suitable heads. Thus, you can improve the presentation generally, while you enlist the entire table of contents in the overall sales effort the proposal represents.

Conformance or Response Matrix

A response matrix is designed to help the reader verify the total responsiveness of your proposal and so maximize your technical score. In general, it is a table that lists the requirements specified in the RFP (derived from the checklists prepared earlier), and assuming the general form shown below. A response matrix is a tabular organization in which are listed all the individual requirements specified in the RFP and SOW, identifying the response to each in your proposal.

Strategy of the Response Matrix

Preparing a response matrix can be tedious, requiring that you first draw up a complete list of all the items to which your proposal must respond—each item of information required, that is. It can run many pages. However, part of the job is done already by the checklists you drew up earlier (see Chapter 2) to help you analyze the requirement and plan your proposal. (You should have drawn up those lists with their later use in a response matrix in mind.) Now you can make additional use of those lists.

Overall, the matrix can help you strategically in at least two ways: One, it helps you ensure that you respond totally to the RFP by providing you with a checklist, thus compelling you to address every item you have previously identified in your lists and/or flowcharts and thus safeguarding you against oversights and inadvertent exclusions that can result in disqualification. (It is thus a vaccine against that most common proposal disease, "nonresponsiveness," which so often proves fatal.) But it also helps by providing the customer—the customer's proposal evaluators, that is—irrefutable evidence that yours is a total and complete response to the RFP. In fact, it compels them to verify that, while drawing attention to the fact that you have done a most thorough job. (I have found that proposal evaluators have occasionally missed noting required responses if they were not guided to those responses.) Where there is numerical scoring of technical proposals, as in federal procurement, the matrix tends to help you earn a maximum score, which improves your prospects overall. And in so doing, it is also an effective competitor strategy, for it tends to overshadow competitors who do not go to the considerable effort required to produce a response matrix.

Aside from the general favorable impact of such a complete and detailed presentation, this tends strongly to maximize your technical score, where the client performs such formal evaluations of proposals, and, in any case, it presents an excellent image.

The presentation is normally along the lines of the figure below (Figure 9.2). The location—page and/or paragraph numbers—of those required items are listed in the leftmost column, and they are identified by brief text in the next column. The specific response made in the proposal is then cited, and an additional column is supplied for notes. This column is available for any notes or remarks you wish to make about the item or about your response to it, but it can be left blank for the client to use in reviewing the proposal and its response matrix. Or you can supply still another column for the use of the client.

Note that it may be necessary to list requirements mentioned in more than one place in the RFP/SOW, and you may have to respond more than once in your proposal. The form lends itself to that multiple notation.

Note, also, that some requirements do not require a textual response of any kind, but assure the customer that you did note those items. The word "Acknowledged" is used to provide that assurance.

The following example of such a presentation is drawn from an actual proposal and reflects one proposer's application of the idea—to a military procurement, in this case. (The items were selected to illustrate the several different cases; the original matrix is actually nine pages long.)

Proposal Back Matter and Sales Strategies

All formal proposals normally have at least some front matter, a title page, table of contents, and executive summary. Back matter normally includes some or all of the following items:

- Bibliographies
- Articles or other papers cited earlier
- Exhibits
- Photos and/or other additional illustrations
- Additional résumés

Figure 9.2   Matrix Showing Compliance with Mil-I-28892A(EC)

Para.	Specification Title/Subject	Proposal Reference Par./Other	Page No.
1.	Scope	Acknowledged	
1.2	Applicable documents	Acknowledged	
3.1	General	2.0	2-1
3.1.1	First article	2.5.3.5	2-65
4.1.1	Weight	Table 2-1	2-5
3.6.6.2	Controls and indicators	2.2, Figure 2-1	2-19, 2-4

If professional papers, articles, passages from books, and other external material is cited in the proposal, it may be a good idea to furnish a complete bibliography in an appendix to lend weight to the "proof" elements of what the proposal promises. However, you may find it even more helpful to present an appendix containing the complete text of whatever materials you have cited in your proposal, as even firmer support of proof. (This may not be possible in a page-limited proposal.)

By the same reasoning, you may have drawings, photographs, or other illustrations that would be of interest to some of your readers, but not all, and may present those in an appendix, which many proposal writers refer to and label as an exhibit.

Some proposal writers supply additional résumés in an appendix to the proposal, rather than in the section that presents the organization's credentials as a contractor. This is a matter of choice, given that the whole idea of an appendix is to present material that would be of interest to some readers, but not to all. The material thus must not be essential to a complete understanding of what is proposed; readers should not be compelled to read it.

A Summary Reminder/ Collection of Key Tips, Solutions, and Strategic Ideas

Many of the strategies and special ideas that were offered and explained in the foregoing pages will be directly applicable to situations you encounter and many will not fit your needs directly. But tips and reminders of the strategic principles should stimulate your creative cells and help inspire you to the invention of many brilliant new strategies from your own imagination. The purposes of this chapter are to help you find the appropriate ideas for the need at hand, to introduce a few strategic ideas that were not mentioned in earlier pages, and to expand on some that were mentioned only briefly earlier and that merit closer examination. There will also appear in this chapter a number of additional examples of basic strategic ideas and how they were implemented. Those "for instances" are sometimes even more helpful than understanding the principle underlying the stratagem.

You may thus regard the collection of ideas presented in this chapter as a kind of checklist or reminder to help you recall them easily and perhaps to become more inculcated with their essential principles. Whichever the case, a main purpose is to provoke and stir your own creative brain cells. Most of us have a much greater creative capability than we make use of; there is ample evidence that it exists and that it can be provoked and stimulated. The collection here is a potpourri of stratagems, some old, some new, but all of them tried and true. They probably will not often be amenable to direct transplantation to your own proposals, of course, but they can often be adapted to your special needs. As you encounter a few new ideas here and refresh your memory of some you have read about before, think about the ways in which you can add your own special twist and make them your own.

There is no particular order here. Read this chapter occasionally for inspiration, especially when you are preparing to tackle a new proposal and can use a bit of mental stimulation. Use it also to search out some specific ideas to help you create a new USP or other strategic initiative. But first read it to refresh yourself on the simple basics of sales strategy.

The Basic Sales/Advertising Strategy

Advertising and selling are based on the principles of proof and promise, a much simpler and more dynamic idea than the often used AIDA—Attention, Interest, Desire, and Action. Promise is first, and it is first because that is what we all sell in every case. We promise, directly or by implication, that what we sell will *do* something for the buyer. It will help the buyer get a better job, make more money, pay less tax, be healthier, be more attractive to the opposite sex, lose weight, be more loved by others, be more secure, be happier, enjoy greater prestige, or enjoy any of a thousand other possible benefits, most with a distinct emotional appeal. We then offer evidence that we can and will deliver on these promises by offering logical arguments, certifications, endorsements by famous people, testimonials by happy customers, assurances by recognized authorities, and sundry other means of "proving" that our diet pills, training program, or kitchen detergent will work as promised and deliver the benefit we promised. Is that not what all those TV commercials do—promise you something and then show you why you can believe the promise?

These marketing/sales ideas are adaptable to proposals which are themselves sales presentations, of course. This entire book has been about how the overall marketing strategy represented by these principles is adapted to and implemented in proposals. Bear in mind always that whatever strategies you employ, they are for a purpose that is in direct or indirect support of these principles. A USP may be conceived to point to and dramatize a promise, for example, as in Ford Motor Company's "better idea" slogan of a few years ago or in a supermarket chain's "Customer's Bill of Rights," intended as evidence to support their promise that they care about their customers. If you keep in mind that all the strategies and related ideas you conceive and use are for the purpose of supporting your promises and proofs, you will more easily grasp the strategic ideas and develop new strategic initiatives of your own. Incidentally, the Ford slogan was a USP, but it was a weak sales appeal because it was about Ford, a self-serving brag about Ford, in fact, and not about the customer, as it should have been. General Electric made the same mistake in using a slogan that said that progress was their most important product, and then they were forced to endure widespread jests that progress was their most important *problem*.

The USP

The USP or Unique Selling Point is a basic strategic idea that is a valuable device in all sales situations, including proposals. It is not used nearly enough, possibly because it is not as well understood as it ought to be, and possibly because it is hard work to develop really effective USPs. Too often, an ordinary logo or slogan is assumed to be a USP, or one continues to use a once effective USP that has outlived its usefulness and no longer qualifies as a USP.

A USP must be memorable and motivating, as well as unique. However, "unique," in this application, is a relative term, one that must be qualified, not one with absolute meaning. The qualification is this: The USP must be unique only in terms of the customer's perception. (In marketing, all truth is whatever the customer perceives as truth.)

Being unique is a requirement of the USP, but not the sole requirement. It must also be something dramatic or novel enough to attract notice and be effective in motivating the customer to want what you offer. A USP has some value in having even one of these qualities, but its maximum value lies in having all these qualities. Even better, the ideal USP also makes a promise to the customer, directly, if possible, but certainly by clear implication. Achieving at least some of these qualities is what represents the true challenge in creating an effective USP.

Unfortunately, most USPs are highly perishable. One reason for this is because competitors are imitative, and the more successful the USP, the more likely it is that competitors will imitate it so that it is no longer unique. But even an unimitated USP gets stale with prolonged use and no longer attracts attention after a time. Keeping USPs fresh and creating new ones, as necessary, are a constant challenge to your imagination in exploiting the USP strategy. Each proposal ought to have its own main USP, but it may and should have USPs for the various elements of the proposal—create a USP for your introduction, another for your discussion, and yet another for the cost proposal or other elements.

The Failure Probability Analysis, mentioned originally in another connection, was such a USP, used as the main USP for the proposal in which it was introduced. But another USP in a proposal offering to design a maintenance plan, offered a concept the customer found controversial—it stated that for maintenance purposes, a component was either good or bad, and never in any state between the two extremes. The position was taken to minimize the need for decision making by maintenance technicians who were not to be highly trained and needed only a go/no-go system. It was a USP that drew attention easily enough, but it also drew opposition as a new and different approach—engineering minds hated what they regarded as oversimplification—and so the idea had to be sold to the customer's engineers. The opposition, however, was a plus, helping to make it a USP because it drew attention, as well as fire, from opponents of the idea.

In yet another case, the customer was concerned about training maintenance technicians and then losing their trained technicians to other organizations, where the individual could earn a higher salary. Here, the winning proposal strategy was to narrow the training to specialize in only the equipment used by that customer's organization, with no general theory training for entry-level maintenance technicians. Advanced training was to be given only to established technicians after a period of service. Again, it was controversial to so limit basic training because it was a radical change from conventional thinking, but it addressed the customer's problem of losing trained technicians.

Running Heads and Feet

Repetition is one element that works to make advertising effective. A first impression does not usually penetrate deeply enough into a prospect's consciousness to result in a sale, but repetition of that impression does tend to do so. In many sales campaigns—in direct mail, for example—repeated mailings to the same list may produce more sales on the third, fourth, or later mailings than on the first one. The same idea is used in broadcast commercials, of course, with some slogans becoming so familiar that they become common usage, as in "Where's the beef?" and "Please, Mother, I'd rather do it myself"— two lines from TV commercials of the past that many people were quoting wryly as humor.

One way to make this principle of repeated appearance work for you in proposals is via the wise use of running heads and feet.

Most published books have running heads, and many have running feet. Those are the captions or brief lines of type that appear at the head or foot of each page in the book, above or below the main text on the page. Probably the most common usage of heads and feet in book publishing is to reproduce the title of the book or the chapter at the head of each left-hand (even-numbered) page, and the title of the chapter or of the principal paragraph at the head of the right-hand (odd-numbered) page. In book publishing, use of heads, rather than feet appears to be favored, and usually one or the other, not both, is used. However, that is book publishing, not proposals and marketing, and you may make whatever use you wish of this idea. And you should make use of it, taking maximum advantage of the possibilities. In fact, it may be of material assistance in conforming with the mandates of the RFP that limits the number of pages you may have in your proposal. (See Chapter 6.)

Today's computers make it easy to insert heads and feet automatically. You can and should put this capability to good use in your proposals. You can run appropriate slogans or other reminders throughout your proposal. You can use both heads and feet on the pages, and you can vary them according to page numbers, sections or chapters, or paragraphs. In this way, you can use a USP for the entire proposal and perhaps another for each section. It is an excellent way to stress your

USP and other sales arguments. Encourage everyone connected with the proposal directly or indirectly to offer slogans and all other ideas to find the most effective ones for heads and feet in your proposals. In fact, the quest for good ideas may be an excellent subject for a brainstorming session. *The captions should say something of note.*

There is a downside. After a while, seeing the same captions on each page, the reader begins, consciously or unconsciously, to ignore the captions and no longer sees them. That is an argument for varying the captions. Change them often, according to the section or main topic you are working with at the moment and the strategy you are using there. If you use captions to identify the main paragraph of the page by repeating the paragraph caption as a header, for example, you will want to be sure that you use paragraph captions that are sales arguments, and you use many new paragraph captions. Devise a system that compromises between mind-numbing repetition and fleeting appearances so that there is both repetition and variety.

Blurbs, Glosses, and Sidebars

There are many ways you can use the capabilities of your computer to create attention-getting effects and deliver special messages. Some other devices for delivering brief, high-impact messages are the blurb and the gloss, brief statements used in various ways. A gloss is a little abstract or note in the margin of a page that summarizes or adds some relevant remark to the text next to it. Usually, there is at least one gloss on a page, and often there are several. Like headlines, glosses can and should be used to help sell the proposal by focusing on benefits and proofs.

A blurb is very much like a gloss, except that it is not used as frequently, and is thus somewhat broader in scope and, usually, of greater length. A blurb generally appears after a major headline or chapter title. Like headlines and glosses, blurbs should be used to sell, as well as to sum up information and communicate generally. See Figure 10.1 for an example of one usage of a blurb, taken from *The Complete Guide to Consulting Contracts.*

Figure	
10.1	**A First Page with a Blurb Under the Title**

Chapter 1

What Is a Contract?

If contracts were truly agreements, they would not end up in bitter court battles, as they so often do.

LAY AND LEGAL DEFINITIONS

It is easy and yet difficult to define the term "contract." The layperson is likely to use a common term, such as "agreement" as a definition, and visualize or refer to a written instrument in using the term. Legal experts tend to shun such one-word definitions as dangerous oversimplification and will explain to anyone who inquires that what is on paper is a statement of the agreement, rather than the agreement or contract itself. To avoid the hazard of misleading simplification, legal minds use and prescribe the use of many clarifying and qualifying terms, including promises, offer, acceptance, consideration, meeting of the minds, and assent, among still others, many of them bearing special meanings for the legal mind. There is also the matter of common law (also known as case law) in comparison to or contrast with statutory law, as the two legal bases affect the governance and enforceability of contracts. The question of enforceability of contracts is obviously an important factor lying at the very heart of the idea of contracting, and we will encounter references to it and discussions of it again and again.

Figure 10.2   Shading to Draw Special Attention to a Sidebar

> Sidebars are another matter, but are also ways to deliver messages to which you draw special attention. In traditional journalistic practice, a sidebar is a story or article that is supplemental to a main story or article. In book publishing, sidebar stories are often printed against a gray screen to distinguish them from the main text.

Sidebars are another matter, but are also ways to deliver messages to which you draw special attention. In traditional journalistic practice, a sidebar is a story or article that is supplemental to a main story or article. In book publishing, sidebar stories are often printed against a gray screen to distinguish them from the main text. (See Figure 10.2 for an example.)

Since computers and word processors make it easy to use such devices as shading, there is no reason not to use the device as a means for highlighting important elements of your proposal to which you want to draw special attention. They depend at least in part on their novelty to draw special attention, so be highly discriminating in selecting those messages you will impart via such devices. Also, if you are photocopying your pages, you need to know the special effects copy well.

There are other ways you can make use of your computer's capability for attention-getting devices by interesting layouts. Figure 10.1, for example, illustrated one way to introduce a sidebar, but there are

| Figure 10.3 | A Typographical Variation for Different Effect |

Chapter 1

What Is a Contract?

LAY AND LEGAL DEFINITIONS

It is easy and yet difficult to define the term "contract." The layperson is likely to use a common term, such as "agreement" as a definition, and visualize or refer to a written instrument in using the term. Legal experts tend to shun such one-word definitions as dangerous over-simplification and will explain to anyone who inquires that what is on paper is a statement of the agreement, rather than the agreement or contract itself. To avoid the hazard of misleading simplification, legal minds use and prescribe the use of many clarifying and qualifying terms, including promises, offer, acceptance, consideration, meeting of the minds, and assent, among still others, many of them bearing special meanings for the legal mind. There is also the matter of common law (also known as case law) in comparison to or contrast with statutory law, as the two legal bases affect the governance and enforceability of contracts. The question of enforceability of contracts is obviously an important factor lying at the very heart of the idea of contracting, and we will encounter references to it and discussions of it again and again.

If contracts were truly agreements, they would not end up in bitter court battles, as they so often do.

for example, illustrated one way to introduce a sidebar, but there are many other ways you can do it easily, as in Figure 10.3.

Actually, using dramatic or attention-getting devices to draw special attention to your most cogent points helps sell your ideas by sheer impact of the presentation. There are two other excellent reasons for using these devices:

1. They make reading and understanding your proposal easier because they act as guidelines, especially to your most important points.
2. They relieve the tedium. (Bear in mind that the reader is faced with reading your proposal as only one of many.)

Such attention-getting devices mean your entire proposal tends to stand out from the crowd and be much more memorable. It is thus a good idea to have someone on the proposal team who is proficient in desktop publishing, especially in layout and typography.

When to Deliver Your Proposal

I have always recommended, as a general rule, that you deliver your proposal to the client as close to the last minute as possible. There are at least two reasons for this advice:

1. It is fairly common for those who issue RFPs to announce an amendment to the Statement of Work or to extend the due date for proposals shortly before the original due date. This creates for you an immediate dilemma if you have already delivered your proposal: Shall you withdraw and retrieve your proposal to make changes or should you pass up the opportunity to gain the extra time so you may again review your proposal closely and possibly strengthen it in some way? You avoid the possibility of a dilemma of this sort by using every minute you have to polish your proposal before delivering it.

2. Frequently, when you deliver a proposal—especially when you deliberately engineer the ploy to arrive at the last minute—you get an opportunity to see the stacked-up proposal packages, even encountering competitors delivering their proposals, and so get an idea of who else has submitted a proposal and is an active competitor for the contract. (Admittedly, with growing delivery of documents by electronic means, this may become far less a consideration than it has been in the past.) This kind of scrutiny has been the basis for successful protests.

These are both good enough reasons to try to manipulate your delivery to make it happen as close to deadline as possible without taking undue risks of the fatal flaw of being late. But there are always exceptions to a general rule, and there is most certainly such an exception here: when your proposal comprises an unusual package. For example, when we included several three-by-four-foot charts with our proposal, we wrapped it all together in a "plain brown wrapper" with the word "PROPOSAL" prominent on the outside. We then delivered our proposal as many days before the deadline as we could manage. The oversize package then stood *prominently* in the client's office, awaiting the day when the deadline had passed so the proposals could be opened. And so for a number of days before our proposal package could be opened, it aroused widespread speculation about what could be contained in the only three-by-five-foot proposal ever seen in that office (or probably, any other office). Our organization thus became well known in that agency before long. We could never be passed over for lack of visibility. And, of course, the staff could not later resist the temptation to call us in to discover what kind of people we were who could contrive and carry out such an outrageous approach.

You could, of course, make this a standard practice. That would not be difficult to do. It would then become an ongoing USP until it became a stale idea. (It would, in time.) Of course, the more success you met with this approach, the more your competitors will be tempted to emulate your example, despite the natural reluctance to say, "Me, too." Your USP would then not be unique any longer and so would not be a true USP. In the meanwhile, it would have done its job. And being the imaginative and resourceful people that you are, you will by then have devised another USP that will demand attention and respect.

Why It Can't Be Done

It is no secret that almost every inventor has had to face the ridicule of "experts" who "knew" that the inventor was a fool headed for certain disaster. Robert Fulton, Louis Pasteur, Thomas Edison, Charles Kettering, and the Wright brothers, to name just a few, were dismissed as misguided individuals who were too ignorant to know that they were pursuing the impossible.

This suggests a means for testing any proposed plan that is even slightly innovative. Many proposal-writing organizations employ "red teams" or "murder boards" to review their proposals with maximum skepticism, as a preview and insight to the most difficult review and valuation they may expect. This arms the proposal team in advance and sets the stage for the final rewrite/polish to meet all possible objections and rebuttals to the arguments in their proposals.

Another, more sharply focused devil's advocate check on a proposal draft is a why-it-can't-be-done review. Individuals expert in the subject matter of the proposal and the customer's RFP presentation review the draft manuscript and develop arguments that demonstrate or "prove" that the proposed plan is fundamentally flawed.

The proposal team, now aware of the possible arguments of the skeptics, must refine the plan and develop counter arguments to refute the anticipated can't-be-done rationales. This strengthens the proposal, and is probably even more important in preparing the key proposal people for the negotiation, where they will probably have to argue the merits of their proposed project.

The "Yes, But" Strategy

Those whose position vis-à-vis anything new seems to always be that it is a foolish idea often have no good reason to cite for their views. Others often have what appears to be a good rationalization. Naysayers command attention, given the common tendency to accept change only reluctantly, and reject completely revolutionary change. The arguments of those who oppose new ideas can be refuted with logic. One of the most common and least logical arguments advanced by those opposed to a new idea is that it has never been done before. The logical response to that is that every advance is something that has never been done before. Two hundred years ago, people had never driven an automobile; a hundred years ago, we could not send pictures through the air. However, for purposes of persuasion, that's the wrong answer, for logic that refutes another strongly held belief tends to polarize the discussion, rather than to persuade. The better strategy here is the "Yes, but" strategy. This is a strategy that avoids confrontation and preserves reasonable discussion instead of a clash of views. It says, "You are right, of course, but consider this," and is then followed by a reasonable explanation that demonstrates that the new idea is not really revolutionary, but is a logical evolution of familiar ideas. The case offered as an example was the offer to create a new system for planning maintenance of equipment via a "failure probability analysis," which was to be a twist on the already well-accepted reliability analysis and its measures. The presentation in the proposal explained the proposed new system in step-by-step detail, carefully showing its evolution from and close relationship to the standard reliability analysis in all facets proposed.

Coping with Vague Work Statements

The vague, rambling Statement of Work is one of the more common and more difficult problems proposal writers face. But there is, as usual, a flip side to this problem. It is a problem that offers special opportunities if you take full advantage of it. The critical element that is usually lacking in this kind of SOW is detailed specification. That puts the burden on you to provide a specification of enough detail to protect yourself against unreasonable demands for which the contract would offer no help or risk disputes that will almost surely cost you dearly to settle. It also offers you the opportunity to set the standard—obviously you would pick one you can easily meet. The general approaches suggested for responses to this problem, depending on the nature of the RFP, include these:

- Two-phase program, first phase to establish work plan/specifications
- Alternative proposals to ensure responsiveness but offer better plan
- Alternative proposals to offer both a minimum configuration to meet goal, and a more advanced plan
- Joint development (with the customer) of work plan/specifications

Principal tools for both making sense of vague SOWs and developing one or more sensible responses include the functional flowchart and lists of whatever is stated as required in the proposal and project design. Mastery in creating functional flowcharts is therefore one of the most valuable talents a proposal writer can have and use. I know of no more effective tool for coping with a vague SOW, or even with a clear one that happens to have gaps in critical information or in specifications. This need to provide your own specification of work and product, if it was lacking or incomplete in the original work statement, is an especially important consideration to avoid disputes or, at least, to provide you a defense against unreasonable demands that result in disputes.

You may see this as a risky proposition, but it is not if you are careful to base your asking price on the specifications you propose. You need not hesitate to offer your own specifications or to make the estimates you need to create specifications. What those specifications are, in fact, is a statement of what you are prepared to commit yourself to for the price you have offered. The client is free to disagree with your estimates, of course, which then makes those estimates—and your price—a proper matter for negotiation. But that is to your benefit, of course, for you are now at a step in which the implication is clear enough that should you succeed in reaching agreement with the client, you will have a contract to sign! Thus, the vague Statement of Work means two things:

- It means that you will have to work hard to develop the details that should have been in the RFP, but weren't.
- It also means that your self-described specifications are almost sure to give you an edge and put you in a strong position to negotiate the contract.

That sums up what this entire book has been about: using imagination, resourcefulness, and hard work—with an unrelenting focus on winning—to win that contract!

Index

About the Author

Herman Holtz, a veteran of the defense and space engineering era as a corporate executive (marketing director), is a proposal consultant. He has written successful proposals for such organizations as Volt Information Sciences, Hercules Corporation, Dun & Bradstreet, U.S. Industries, and other prominent corporations, and has won contracts with such clients as the FAA, Labor Department, Energy Department, and military departments. *Proven Proposal Strategies to Win More Business* is one of more than 60 how-to books he has written about marketing and other business activities.